Confessions of a Deputation Missionary

Melissa Brown

Published by Melissa Brown, 2013.

CONFESSIONS OF A DEPUTATION MISSIONARY

First edition. December 8, 2013.

ISBN: 979-8224660308

Written by Melissa Brown.

Confessions of a Deputation Missionary
(A Memoir)
by Melissa A. Brown
Smashwords Edition
Copyright 2013 Melissa Brown

Confessions of a Deputation Missionary
(A Memoir)
By Melissa A. Brown

Prologue- An Introduction

The plan seemed simple enough. We pack. We drive. We speak and share. We go. Little did we know, *deputation* for God's missionaries in the 21st century is heavily seasoned by drama, tears, rejection, annoyance, joy, laughter, and welcome (and that's probably just in the first week or two).

I was raised in a small independent Baptist church, pastored by my dad. So when my husband, called to be a church planting missionary in Australia, said we would be working with a Baptist fellowship (basically a network of like-faith churches) and a mission agency (a family of missionaries and an office through which monies can be legally administered), I had no idea what that actually meant. I had never seen pastors gather on a regular basis for solidarity and fellowship. I had all the experience in the world at working within the church and its local ministries, but collaboration of churches on a regular basis was rather foreign.

Our first experience with the fellowship should have given us a clue that deputation wouldn't be predictable or boring. It was fall of 2009. Mission Camp (sounds really fun, right?). Deep in the forest of Oklahoma. 100+ degrees outside. Gnats and mosquitoes buzzing relentlessly. Still considered newlyweds at the time, my husband and I only packed one bag for the three day trip, only to arrive and learn we'd been given sleeping quarters in two different buildings (one dorm for the guys and one for the girls). Really? Would've been nice to get that memo earlier. Okay. No problem. We're adaptable (the soon to be ABSOLUTE MANTRA of our lives). Next stop, interview time with the mission board. Two innocents facing a firing squad of fifteen guns. Anxiety builds...okay, so it wasn't quite that bad, but intimidating certainly to sit before a group of fifteen pastors, feeling insecure like a child who hasn't actually done anything wrong but is sure he'll somehow be in trouble anyway. Interview over, an audible sigh of relief sounds through the trees, a final verdict of denial or acceptance the only remaining piece to the puzzle of preparation before publicly starting deputation. It wasn't until the evening service that the mission board finally chose to let the hammer fall. We all had good jobs, they said. There is a recession making deputation difficult, they said. Faces were visibly becoming pale, and tears were welling up in the eyes of the anxious. It was about to be the worst week ever! Trepidation and disbelief warred for predominance in my mind until, "Because of all those things, we will be welcoming each of you into the family of missionaries, approving all of you to begin deputation." Heartbeats started again, and all of a sudden collective breaths we hadn't even known we were holding flooded into the air, now filled with smiles and applause. I barely registered the conspiratorial, teasing expressions of the mission board as relief beat out the thoughts that had been running through my mind. Now, the hard part, *DEPUTATION*. And so, the journey begins.

CHAPTER ONE- Booking Appointments

After our hazing at mission camp, we truly felt a part of the fellowship family and were incredibly excited about the process of traveling and sharing our call with all the churches we possibly could. Naïve zeal is a wonderful, needful, yet tenuous part of any young person's endeavors. I, for one, had all kinds of ideas about how to be successful on deputation. Well, you simply make hundreds of calls a day if that's what it takes. Right? Well, apparently, not always. One of the most difficult things as a missionary wife is that I cannot help my husband in that department. There are plenty of things that I do on a daily basis and fully care for regarding our ministry, but calling churches and making appointments is strictly my husband's job. Though I totally understand this, it still can feel frustrating when people advise that a missionary simply make more calls (play the numbers game), but one person can only make so many calls by himself. That's how it is, and that's how it will remain. Okay. We're adaptable.

Booking appointments is job ONE during deputation, be in as many churches as you possibly can in the shortest possible time. After all, back in the hey day of foreign missionaries in the U.S., missionaries were often able to book three appointments each week, being in a different church for each service, all year long, some getting to field after only eighteen months of busy deputation. The 21st century, however, has a vastly different climate for deputation missionaries. In my mind, I sometimes refer to the 21st Century as the Ice Age of Biblical missions, appropriately named because many people and churches have become increasingly cold to mission work and those who are called to it. The reasons why pastors have declined to give an appointment are usually understandable and legitimate, sometimes frustrating, and sometimes downright hypocritical. Sometimes it blows my mind the things that pastors will say to get out of making an appointment with a missionary. Of course, that is only if a pastor actually answers his phone or takes the time to return a message. Fewer than 10% of the calls a missionary makes even result in a conversation with a pastor, let alone an appointment.

Anyone who has ever been involved in fund raising can tell you that many elements must come together seamlessly in order to complete the job successfully. Sometimes those elements are clearly delineated (like it makes sense that a church that disagrees with a missionary on basic doctrine will not support that missionary); sometimes those elements include highly subjective unwritten rules that the missionary may only happen upon unwittingly (like the pastor who canceled our appointment when he learned that I wore regular slacks outside of church). Many pastors are extremely gracious and friendly and provide missionaries with honesty and respect. The not-so-honest ones, however, truly provide some grimaces as well as occasional groans.

The level of creativity among clergy jumps exponentially when they are faced with a missionary seeking an appointment. Let's see, there was the pastor who would only wear jeans (not shorts) while swimming in the ocean; there was the one who said that no first world countries (only the 10:40 window) needed missionaries. Some say they cannot support missionaries who use a mission agency (Yes, our agency is clearly shady; those ladies who help keep all of our funding legal and organized for simple, clear tax returns are not interested in God's work at all) as opposed to missionaries who deposit the 100+ checks per month into private bank accounts and keep tax records solely on their own. Yes, that one is always a favorite! Some pastors purposefully ask completely inappropriate questions (like what you wear to bed or how often your marriage enjoys itself...if you get my drift), presumably seeking some specific answer but really just using it as a subversive technique that effectively cancels a missionary's desire to visit them as well as their responsibility then to support God's work. I've heard of pastors who refuse support when a missionary couple has no children and/or have too many children. Some pastors, located near famous landmarks, refuse to see missionaries who even consider taking an off day to see national monuments or spend real family time with their children. Some pastors say they do not make appointments over the phone (effectively negating 99% of missionary attempts to speak with them); some limit appointments to a specific number per year (booking an entire year in the span of a few minutes and a few missionaries). We've even had church secretaries reveal that they've received special instructions (missionaries mentioning *deputation* are not allowed an audience with the pastor, while missionaries on *furlough* [already been on their field working] can be put through without difficulty). There are the churches who simply refuse to participate in foreign missions (great commission simply ignored), and there are those who choose to support only missionaries associated with specific fellowships. These are all real reasons, to be sure, but I prefer to be honest with myself in all things; most No's are simply excuses for inactivity and unbelief on the part of the local church.

Amazingly enough, though excuses abound, God proves Himself even more creative in meeting each of our needs, regardless of how uniquely rebuffed we may be by churches. Plenty of pastors and church members truly love God and honestly want to see His work done throughout the world. We have had the privilege of participating in many services in which God's mission of reaching the world is highlighted and honored. What never ceases to amaze is God's resourcefulness in getting us where He wants us in the time He wants.

No matter what we encounter, we've seen one thing reinforced time and time again: God is Sovereign over all, and His will proceeds with or without human assistance! Sobering to some; refreshing and encouraging to us. My husband may go two or three weeks with no appointments booked; then he has days like today and books three within the span of a couple of hours. These are moments of reassurance, times when we can refocus on why we do what we do, why we travel thousands of miles every month, why we live out of an SUV, why our daughter has never had a crib, why my husband spends tens of hours on the phone each week, why we work so hard to connect with God's people.

Booking appointments is job one for a missionary. Without appointments, we don't have much chance of sharing God's call on our lives. Without appointments, we don't have much chance of partnering with the people of God in God's work. Without appointments, churches do not have the opportunity to fulfill their part in the Great Commission. Without appointments, we cannot do what God has called us to do. Though creative excuses abound, God's provision through His people and through methods we cannot even imagine yet provides the standard of His faithfulness in which we have so much faith.

Chapter Two- Always a Visitor, Never the Bride (Er...Family)

Few things epitomize the nomadic, unsettled existence of missionaries on deputation like the varied experiences of corporate worship while traveling. Now, anyone who knows the Bible will tell you that worship itself includes all aspects of our lives (our daily walk and talk, everywhere we go, everywhere we are), but corporate worship is that unique coming together of a body of believers for the sake of honoring God as a collective. It is in this corporate atmosphere that arises the concept of our church family. Those who worship together have a familial bond that is beautiful and designed by God to be close and powerful, even symbiotic in nature. Our church family is designed to be a group of people whose separate skills, talents, and callings work together for the edification and betterment of everyone else. I've heard many arguments regarding the validity of God's command to be a faithful, active member of a church body. The purpose here isn't to debate why we should be adhering to a command of God or not (that really should go without saying), but I will say that I have missed worshipping with my church family more than any other thing we've given up during the entire deputation process.

Have you ever been the new kid at school? The rookie on the job? The newest in-law at the family reunion? The neighbor who just moved in down the street? None of these are bad things, in fact, you may even really like the new environment. Hopefully, you'll quickly make friends at the new school. You'll prove your worth as part of the team at work. You'll show them that you love their family, while trying to remember everyone's names and attempting to decipher inside jokes that are probably better left unexplained. You might even get cookies from the local neighborhood watch program as they welcome you warmly into their group of suburbanites. It's not a bad thing to be new.

Sometimes, new can be very nice...like a new car, a new outfit, or that new ice cream flavor at Cold Stone you've been dying to taste.

Imagine driving into a parking lot, small trees lining the perimeter, a brilliantly white cross sitting proudly atop the building's apex. The morning has been busy already, showers and shaves, donning crisp and clean clothing, preparing a quick on-the-go breakfast, brushing a toddler's hair while keeping her little hands from pulling off her dress shoes, all while ensuring that a fully stocked diaper bag and set of Bibles make it to the car at the same time as your family does. The GPS hasn't failed this morning, and you arrive at your destination with plenty of time to spare (in fact, you're not even sure if the pastor is there, as you see no other cars beside yours). You munch the remainder of your breakfast and down some water, while cleaning your toddler's fingers of food particles and putting on her shoes one more time. You barely register the praise song playing on the car radio (it's a favorite, but you haven't been listening and the last chorus is now fading away). Almost too quickly to notice, you sigh. But, you are prepared for the morning services. You have a swanky display board, fun foreign items for people to peruse, and (of course) a flag the people aren't familiar with, so that everyone who sees you will know that you will eventually not be in America any longer. You are going somewhere else, to be part of some other life, some other culture, some other people, some other family. You get out of the car and breathe a prayer of thanksgiving for Sunday mornings, the relative calm of a population largely still asleep and the silence of empty streets. Sundays are blessings, each one a blissful second of stillness in the harried week of work and traffic and extracurricular activities that daily demand our attention. With that in mind, you smile and finish unloading the display board and projector and DVD of pictures, as well as the toddler, diaper bag, and the Bibles, anticipating a wonderful time in God's house with God's people. You inhale the stillness around you, the sweetness of God's presence and His creation, notice the pretty blue and red flowers that dot the church's entryway, and then...you grab your toddler's hand before she can walk into the path of an approaching car. Like many buildings, a church is quiet before the people arrive, no TV's blaring, no car horns honking, no cell phones ringing. The quietness of an empty church is quite a remarkable thing. God inhabits His people, not a physical building, but His still, small voice can sure seem amplified in a lonely sanctuary. As you set up your "missionary stuff," you keep an eye on your exploring child, reminding her not to take out all the offering envelopes from the back of the pews. The choir loft that serves to frame a baptistry catches your eye, and you notice a lovely landscape mural painted behind it (a winding river cascading down into the shadows). The song "Shall We Gather at the River?" begins playing in your mind, like muscle memory, your brain recalling several verses that you sing to your little girl while she laughs and walks up and down the center aisle. Several people have come in the door by this point, and you make a point to greet each one, offering your name and silently repeating their names several times in your head in the hopes that you'll remember them longer than five minutes. It's still 20 minutes until the start of the first service, but you want to know where your child will need to be: does this church have a nursery? Where, O, where is the nursery? You head down a main corridor glancing high and low for any kind of sign that you are walking in the right direction. Is it this way? Is there a nursery worker here yet? You look in every open doorway, finally stumbling upon what you think may be the nursery, pastel walls, a changing table, lots of toys and books. Yep, standard nursery accoutrements. It's empty. No people here yet. You lead your child inside, setting the diaper bag on a white counter top as the colorful animals in the corner find a new playmate. It's a cute room decorated with Noah's arks, lots of color, and lots of animals. Should you stay here in case someone comes, or should you take your chances with a squirmy toddler in the service, sitting close to the back so that you can bow out of the auditorium as only a minimal distraction when your child's attention span doesn't make it through an entire sermon? What to do? You think, will anyone be offended if I'm not in Sunday school, if I'm here with my child keeping her from being a disturbance? What did he say: Are we presenting our ministry during Sunday school or the main service? Man, is there a schedule of nursery workers around here? Several minutes later, a smiling church member is walking toward you, and a big sigh of relief runs down your arms as you realize no decision must be made. You only have a couple minutes until the service is to begin, but at least you won't be missed. As the charming lady glimpses your child, her face fills with delight at the bright "Hi" and grand smile your toddler now gives most strangers, especially people who enter the rooms full of toys found in all these churches you visit. You think about the friends that she'll make that day but wish that she didn't always have to miss the friends she has at your home church. Familiar faces and expected playtime rules are not the norm for her. At least she's young and won't really remember any of this constant traveling. Yet, you wonder what kind of long-term effects it's having on her even now. Hopefully soon, life will be more permanent and stable. Time to go. Child taken care of. Check. Three minutes until the service starts.

Time to start the service, which will be just like any other service, right? After all, most people think that it doesn't matter where they go or what is said. Church is church, right? Mmm, not quite. Yes, the Lord never changes. His Word never changes. His expectations and standards for us never change, but a church is a community made up of unique believers with many skills and talents and natural abilities. It is the special collection of these abilities that when placed together and used for God's glory brings everyone closer to Him and makes everyone better. Without a specific church home, a person's special abilities go unused, and without that specific person, a church goes without a blessing or ability that it was meant to have.

The service starts with a hymn, a common one long held in high regard by the religious community. You listen to the voices as you sing, clearly participating but trying not to be too loud (projecting with volume has never been an issue). You recognize the alto part being sung by a voice near the back, loving the sound of harmony as it pulls out the tremendous beauty in the hymn's melody. Oh, it's so nice when there are people who can sing different parts in a church...and, more importantly, when they are willing to actually do it. The hymn ends, and it's time for the morning announcements. The pastor mentions a few church members who need prayer for physical ailments. You sympathize with those in pain but wish that you knew who he was talking about, knew how they fit into this lovely family that you're only joining temporarily. It makes it much harder to pray for people that you've never met and don't even know what they look like. You send up a prayer for the names listed, wishing there was more you could do and hoping that this church family rallies around those hurting. Prayer requests are followed by the upcoming church events, a youth movie night (how fun is that) and a fellowship for the young marrieds' class (nursery provided...oh yeah!). You remember how much fun you always have getting together with your church family for these types of outings, and you pray that these people know how blessed they are to be able to participate like this. There's a young couple in the third row who glance to the back and smile, you assume at another couple they will be having fun with at the meal. Ah, the joy of being in the family! The pastor then gives a reminder for a marriage conference being held the next month and the cost of tickets for those who've signed up to attend. "For those of you going, make sure you've given your deposit money to Mrs. Smith by next Sunday" (oh, you wish you were giving Mrs. Smith money...that'll be a great weekend). Then, the youth pastor steps up and announces with a 100 watt smile that three young people had accepted Christ as Savior at the youth rally the night before! You feel your own smile expand, your heart bursting with joy for the teens you've never even set eyes on and so excited for the youth pastor able to shepherd them into the fold and praying the adolescents are able to grow in the knowledge of Him and find themselves whole in His love. It's the most awesome thing in the world to be a part of a person's journey to Christ, and it makes you long to be on the field doing just what many of these people are doing in this church each week. The announcements reflect the life of the church, its pains and its joys, its trials and its celebrations. As the next hymn number is called, you wonder what announcements were made at your home church that morning. Are you missing another ladies' meeting or baby shower? Have any more students joined the youth group? How's that precious lady doing who'd been in the hospital that last time you'd heard any word? Have they finished that renovation on the bathrooms? You wish you could have helped with those things, but God has different plans for the moment.

Then comes, customary in many churches, the worship service's time of fellowship, when the pianist keeps playing and people walk around, shake hands, greet each other, and generally fellowship. This time usually results in two things: a traffic jam in the main aisle and the sincere wish that it last longer when the song leader calls people back to their seats to continue singing. Easy and fun when you are with family, pleasant but slightly awkward as a visitor. You smile at every face and shake every hand, even getting the occasional hug, but it's not the same if you are just meeting each face for the first time, just trying to start a bond with people who have long since been bonded to each other. You see a group of ladies on the end of a middle pew, their happy chatter over the plans for an upcoming potluck reaching your ears. You see a little boy run into the legs of an older gentleman, both laughing in shared fun with the ease of habit. As the smiling faces, tender embraces, and endearments surround you, you think of home, the place where every face is known and where life events have been shared, where inside jokes abound and tears have been cried, where everybody knows your name...wasn't there a TV show tune about that? Ah, now it makes sense! These people are great, truly; they just aren't family yet. Hopefully, you can make them family. Hopefully, some will try to get to know you better, keep up with you online, maybe even send a card or two. Hopefully, this won't be the one and only time your life interacts with theirs, but you realize that most churches are just that, people that you meet for one service and never hear from again. You make your way back to your seat as the song leader directs the final verse of the hymn, quietly standing in your row, singing along with the words, trying to recapture the glow of newness that you felt when you came into church that morning, that exciting spark of hope that you would be able to be family with these new people. "Where everybody knows your name..." a few simple bars of an iconic melody float through your mind. No, you don't know many details of the show or its characters, but you definitely get what the song is celebrating. It makes you miss home, but it also makes you consider the family that you will build with people on the other side of the world, people who don't know you or Jesus yet, people who need Him and need you to tell them about Him, so they can be a part of that family as well. That's an exciting thought!

The music comes to an end. Time for the sermon. God's Word. God never changes; therefore, His Word never changes, and it never ceases to amaze how God's Word always has the power to speak to one who is listening, no matter who the messenger may be. You settle in with your Bible on your lap, ready and anxious to hear from Him. Satan, however, wants to pull your mind in all kinds of directions: Was the music on our video okay? Does this church consider your field to be a reached people with no more need for missionaries? Are the things on our display table interesting enough? How many prayer cards are left? Did the kids put the mandatory stuffed animal back on the table? Did your husband answer all the people's questions well enough? Were you clear? Were you passionate? Could the people feel your heart for your field? Could they see the vision that God has given you? Wait, what was the pastor's sermon text again? You glance at your husband who smiles and points to his open Bible. You scramble mentally to catch up, feeling the warmth rising on your face to be caught, if only momentarily, zoned out from the service at hand. Okay, so time for retrospection later. You focus on the pastor's words as he expounds on a familiar passage, reiterating familiar thoughts, your own mind constructing its own Bible study lesson from his text and considering another level to the meaning and application of the scripture. Hmmm, you'd never thought of that verse that way. That would be so helpful to people in this kind of position. You wonder if you'll meet people who struggle with that particularly and realize your mind is wandering again. Yes, pastor, that's a good point, you think to yourself: "Amen" spoken out loud. You promise you are paying attention. God is gracious, and you are thankful that He continues patiently to teach you even if you often have to fight through a mountain of intruding considerations and expectations in order to focus on the lesson. The sermon ends. The soft invitation of an open altar. The silent prayers and soothing strains of the piano playing a hymn of surrender. The lights almost seem dimmer as the air takes on the quietness of soul searching. Bowed heads seek the Lord, together yet separate in their longings, each with different burdens before Him. The benediction prayer is offered, during which is the walk to the auditorium doors, preparing to bid a pleasant adieu to this largely unknown mass of people. You shake hands with all who pass by, wishing them a restful afternoon and fine weather in the coming week. You hand out your prayer cards to all who will take them and thank them for their prayers. You notice a few people walk by without even glancing your way or acknowledging your presence as you engage in conversation with two ladies who've been looking at your display. You see the pastor's wife share a hug with a child and see the affection displayed by most everyone for the group that's been brought together that morning. Yes, church family is a unique and God-designed blessing that you don't take for granted.

Next task, pick up the toddler. You head back to the nursery and, thankfully, are met with plenty of smiles and a little girl running toward the door in her excitement over your return. Then she instantly asks after her dad and wants to go find him as well. The nursery workers give you a rundown of snacks consumed and changes made, noting that "she was so good and did so well." It's the best report, and you are grateful that it's been the norm for your toddler who has been in more nurseries than most kids have changes of clothing. You offer sincere thanks for their service as you take your diaper bag in hand and turn to follow your child who is already half way back to the church's foyer and her daddy who sees her coming and plays a few seconds of peek-a-boo as a teaser before picking her up. All is right with the world in this moment, and you know God has been very good to your little family.

The crowd has largely disappeared by now, only a few straggling friends chatting in various spots, and it's time to pack up. The cards, animals, games, and display board go back in their carry-ons. Time to head out. Your husband gets in a few last words with the pastor, who wishes you all the best and sends his prayers along with you on your journey. You thank him and his wife for their friendly hospitality and welcome, appreciating the good fellowship you've had there. This is another service as a visiting missionary. You know that you will relive this experience again and again as your deputation takes you through dozens of states and hundreds more churches. You are thankful for the blessing of getting to witness so many of God's people truly participating in the family of God that their local church provides them and are thankful for the church family that has sent you to expand the ministry overseas. Being a visitor can be awkward, can be exciting, can be difficult, or it can be nice. God tells us to be more than a visitor in a local body of believers to which we can contribute our unique selves for everyone's benefit. We love meeting God's children all over the country, but nothing compares to the joy, peace, and comfort that exists within a person's home church, their church family. That is why we can't wait to extend our church family onto our field, helping people there learn the wonderful harmony that exists when people are joined by a love for the true God and for each other! It's always a blessing to be at home, though the actual location seldom seems to matter. The old adage says: Home is where the heart is. Are you a visitor? Or are you family?

Chapter Three- We Get to Stay Here?

A "favorite" (and never predictable- you'll understand the air quotes soon enough) aspect to deputation is the incredible variety of living arrangements that missionaries get to experience while on the road. Some comfortable, some questionable, some enviable, and some downright unbelievable, missionary accommodations are as unique to the people and churches providing them as the décor with which they may or may not be accessorized. Sometimes feeling comfortable is easy, sometimes not so much. But, I have found that being able to accomplish the most seemingly mundane things (like laundry and home cooking) can turn a room into a "home" when needed. For that reason, I always use the word home when talking to my daughter about the places we stay. Home creates a sense of stability and belonging. I can still see and feel each of these places in my mind. Remember every person? Sorry. Remember all of the churches? Wish I could. Remember every comfy (or not) bed, broken VCR, and kitchen style? For some crazy reason, yes! Though most are simple, clean places in which we were more than comfortable spending a night or two, several have boasted the kind of eccentricities that render them unforgettable. It's amazing and inexplicable the details our brains will and will not retain from our life experiences, but I can tell you one thing above all: Getting a decent mattress is job ONE when we get a permanent place on the field.

Until I started traveling as a missionary, I'd never even heard of a "prophet's chamber." It's totally Biblical though. II Kings 4 relays the story of a wealthy Shunamite woman who was moved to provide a sparsely, yet very functional, furnished room in her home for the prophet Elisha, a place for him to retire when he was in her area. Many churches have implemented this concept and created such spaces in their church buildings. Generally we have discovered, when a church boasts a prophet's chamber, it almost exclusively refers to a single room within the church, usually adjacent to the kitchen or fellowship hall. A bed, a light, sometimes a desk, sometimes a chair, even a TV (in some really nice ones). How are these chambers different from a "mission apartment" or "mission house" you ask? That is a great question, and the answer is quite simple. Location and amount of space. Now, we have stayed in countless prophet's chambers, and they are usually quite comfortable and practical for a night or a weekend (like a hotel room) but not always ideal for an extended stay. One such chamber, in what appeared to be a lovely little church on the East coast, provided quite the experience for us. That's where I'll begin this adventure for you.

———-

It's evening. We've been driving all day. We are more than ready to get out of the car, get comfy, and fall asleep. Our 9 month old baby girl is getting antsy, done with the straps of her car seat after an eight hour drive. The church parking lot is silent and dark, one street lamp gloomily creating deep shadows along the edge of the sanctuary building. A large gymnasium sits neatly behind the main church building along with a small yet colorfully painted daycare center. The pastor is running late, but we're just content to have arrived safely with no more driving on the agenda. When we finally meet the pastor, he greets us warmly and leads us toward the gymnasium (half the building a gym, the other the church's fellowship hall). We have a prophet's chamber, he informs us (there'd been a promised church kitchen that we'd be able to access as well). I am quite excited about a full kitchen (being able to cook actual meals while traveling full-time is more of a luxury than you'd think). Stepping into the large building, we are met with round, white tables stretching out across an expansive space and a kitchen pass-through in the corner. There are several faux trees and other miscellaneous decorations sitting along the wall, and then the pastor shows us to the prophet's chamber, which will be home for the next month. A single room with a single window. Two high back chairs surrounding a mini brass and glass table with a reading lamp. A brass headboard over a full-size bed jutting out at an angle from the corner. A stand mirror in the corner taking up the only remaining floor space and reflecting the neat yet completely barren walls. Hmmm, simply placing our luggage will be a trick in the limited space, let alone putting up our baby's pack 'n play. It is while on tour of the large kitchen that we are informed about the limitations of the little used room (only the fridge and small microwave are actually in working order). THIS will be an interesting month with a single microwave as our sole culinary appliance (definitely disappointed...it's no wonder so many people struggle to control weight gain while on deputation). The room quiet, the moonlight bright on the other side of the window pane, we bid the pastor good night and set about unloading the car and preparing for much needed sleep. So, there isn't much space, but it isn't anything we can't handle. A silent groan goes through my mind as I spot a third dead bug lying belly up along the wall where I am trying to place the baby bed. The musty smell of old vanilla wafts through the air as if an air freshener had been considered but never quite implemented throughout the space. So, it isn't what we'd thought, but that doesn't negate the blessing of a dry space. Five weeks of cereal, frozen TV dinners, and watching our portable dvd player set on the edge of the bed goes by pretty quickly though. It is there that our daughter begins to crawl, hitting a major milestone and exploring her environment to a whole new level, making me frustrated when she crawls out the bedroom door and finds a dead bug or two on the floor of the fellowship hall, promptly sticking one in her curiosity-driven mouth. Ugh, gross! Thankfully, this too shall (did) pass.

———-

I'd never heard the term F.R.O.G. (finished room over a garage) until my husband kept using it to describe the mission apartment to which we've arrived. Rather than in the church building, this FROG is right beside the church building, a fun new twist. It is February (the coldest month of the year in Texas), and we are happy to find a place to stay, even if our now one year old is beginning to find it difficult to sleep in the same room with us. Other than the true miniature kitchenette in one corner of the room (the stove had only one back and one front burner and an oven no wider than one cookie sheet, with a single sink and counter only large enough for the microwave completing the space), the lack of all bedding (sheets included) on the double bed is the first major red flag. Carrying a set of sheets is part of the deputation gig, so that is no problem. But, I envision the three of us huddled together, teeth chattering, our breath forming foggy streaks across chilled windows, our child turning slightly blue as we struggle for warmth in the frigid winter weather...Okay, so by frigid I mean not quite freezing (it is Texas after all) and by turning blue I mean that our child is bundled in her fuzzy turquoise feety pajamas (they are the BEST), but having no blanket is still not an option. We set out for the local Wal-Mart and buy not only a cozy green, fleece blanket for the bed but also pans and dishes to cook in the completely barren kitchenette. To this day, I can count on my two hands the number of times we've had to pull out those pans, but I've appreciated them every time I've needed them. So, we settle into the FROG (scheduled to spend a month there) and didn't think anything more of the bedding situation until a week later. That next week, it's time to do laundry, and we've been told the church has a washer/dryer set that we are welcome to use during our stay. Yes, I'm always grateful to miss out on the Laundromat. So, I head into the church building, feeling assaulted by a thick musty scent in the air and remembering that the church has been dealing with a water leak and is in the clean-up stages of a mildew explosion. Whew, mildew is certainly a pervasive stench. No worries.

I head away from the smell down a back corridor to the farthest point down the back hallway. As I near the laundry area, a distinct odor begins to waft my way yet again. Ah! I find the culprit and, what's more, the catalyst for the mysterious bedding disappearance. Trying not to breathe too deeply, I discover sheets and a comforter in the washing machine, half dry and half musty with dampness. So someone brought all the linens over from the FROG, started the laundry and never returned. That's been over a week ago...no wonder there is a smell. I put the offensive items into the dryer with some extra scented dryer sheets, and start my own washing. I guess the mildew problem has so permeated the church building that no one wonders about the faint smell coming from the laundry room, including whoever left it there. It's a very cold month, but we stay nice and warm with our new blanket. No one's teeth chattering, and our child's color reflecting only a normal body temperature. Really, what more could we ask for?

———-

Ever wonder what it'd be like to sleep next to your favorite football field? Well, it certainly isn't our favorite (actually, I don't even remember the church's name or the school's mascot), but we're staying in one missions apartment that is literally beside the church's football stadium. Yep. The church not only has a Christian school, but the school has its own football stadium. And, we are lucky enough to be there on a Friday night (just in time for junior varsity to be finishing up their scrimmage as the varsity team prepares for a later game). Hmmm, the secretary said the apartment was on the church property. Could it be that building over there? Is it in the sanctuary building? Which of these buildings is the school part? We do eventually navigate the tide of people and cars in and out of the stadium and discover a small building housing six apartments (3 at floor level, 3 on a 2nd floor). Ah, our destination is one of those. There are random toys and children's bikes strewn about the miniature stretch of lawn in front of the building. A short rope hangs along the chain link fence for the purpose of drying a few pieces of laundry. Dirty, plastic chairs line a span of wall outside one lower-level door while one lies awkwardly beside them. I spy broken mini blinds in three of the windows and wonder who lives in the other apartments and which will be our space for the evening. We find double doors on the lower level accessing a laundry room, used by the whole building. We are only going to be there one night, but it's been several days since I've been able to wash clothes; I'm grateful for the available appliances. The mission apartment is the center door downstairs, right underneath the single metal staircase. A mini one bedroom space covered in dark wood paneling, maybe fifteen square feet of kitchen with a living room only about twice the size of the sofa it held. Dark woods, floral prints, and gilded metal dominate the small space. It takes only minutes to unload the few items that we will need for the evening, and we settle into the space with the lively sounds of an awakened sports arena just outside the door. We can smell the hotdogs from the concession stand and hear the cheerleaders warming up the crowd. I have no idea who won; we don't actually go to the game, but apparently people had a great time because there is plenty of laughter and activity until sometime after 10 that night. I don't remember what time we got to sleep, but I remember that thankfully the next day is not a school day. The parking lot remains blessedly still and quiet long into the next morning, leaving our packing up and moving out an easy, relaxed process. That's always a blessing!

———-

I've never seen a teenier mobile home. We are staying with a lovely, little church, pastored by a wonderful couple who had been foreign missionaries for many years themselves and are full of amazing stories and grand adventures. The mission house is a teeny mobile home sitting in the couple's backyard, with the church building right next door. Now, small spaces are not a big deal; we've been in plenty of small places. Hmm, where to put the baby bed? Ah, there's floor space in front of the kitchen sink. No midnight snacks here (the bed effectively blocked the refrigerator door...as well as everything else in the "living room/kitchenette" area). You think I'm kidding, but ah, that's the fun! There literally is no other open space, but that isn't the really interesting part. What makes this particular home unique besides its size? I'm so glad you're curious! A shocking plethora of knick knacks from around the world, literally, graces every single nook, cranny, shelf, wall, and floor space in the already small apartment. Vases from Asia. Wood elephants from India. Japanese fans on the faux wood paneled walls. Brightly colored, hand woven pillows from Pakistan dance across the retro love seat. The mini fridge is definitely 40's vintage, its cool rounded edges reminiscent of a style and era gone by. The book shelves and counter tops are decorated with dark wood carvings and gilded paintings of scenic locations, creating an atmosphere of cluttered richness. You can travel through the home's décor and spot every mission trip, glimpse each field on which this wonderful couple ever served. Though the home is stuffed to beyond capacity, it screams a life filled with service, worship, and culture, a life fully used for God's glory around the world, a life rich in its scope. How awesome that is!

———-

It is a week-long round robin conference spanning two different states, churches in Colorado and Nebraska. What they don't mention ahead of time is that we'll be sleeping in Wyoming. Yep, in a retreat center set into the plains of Wyoming surrounded by wandering Bison and deer. Fortunately, we're sharing the place with two other families who are in the conference with us. Initially, they have us girls separated from the boys in the segregated camp-style dorm rooms, but we soon redistribute ourselves into families, making the sleeping arrangements much more comfortable (as each family takes a room). We do, however, keep the restrooms segregated to the boys and girls (most of the time). It's simpler that way. Also, since our daughter takes afternoon naps and goes to bed earlier than everyone else, it is definitely more convenient for the other girls not to share bedroom space with a baby. A classic retreat/camp environment, our room holds about twenty bunk beds as well as two futons sitting in the center of the room. The walls are concrete, and the floor is cold cement. We do what all junior campers wish they could do and stack two of the thin plastic mattresses on each of our beds for extra cushion to sleep on. The bathrooms house plastic stall showers and multiple toilets separated by only thin plywood walls and plastic shower curtains for privacy. Ah, I remember being in junior high at summer camp, half the girls trying to sleep past the counselor's blaring alarm while the other half fight for space in front of the bathroom mirrors to dry and curl their hair. The smell of bleach cleaner permeates the air, and my feet (sans shoes) begin to feel the early March chill in the cement floors. With the car unloaded, it's time to take it all in. Outside the camp's main building lies a picturesque landscape, rolling plains as far as the eye can see, broken only by a slight smattering of trees, the train track running just outside the property line, and the lone two-lane road meandering away from the camp and over the hills. Inside the building, the central great room holds a television corner seating area, a set of couches surrounding a fireplace in another corner, lots of open floor space, and six round white tables next to the giant pass-through into the large utility kitchen. The evening before the conference begins (the only relaxing moments we actually spend at the retreat center), the sounds of chatter and video game play echo around the large room, each noise seeming to bounce playfully around the cement space. Dinner is made, and fellowship is had. Our daughter comes up with two new favorite sounds to repeat ad nauseam (B-I-B-I-B-I and ArdeeArdeeArdee), which delights her adopted family (the other deputation missionaries to whom we've become close). It's a wonderful and rare treat spending time with friends, and we thoroughly enjoy the quality time. Only the shrieking sound of a train whistle periodically disturbs the retreat environment; conductors make a point of loudly blowing their horns at all hours of the day and night, presumably to warn off the many buffalo that make a habit of lounging across the train tracks. Oh, no buffalo splayed on the railroad crossing? So no, I have no idea why it is imperative that all conductors blast the most obnoxious sound ever into the silent night when there is not a living thing in sight. At least a box fan on the floor in the dormitory seems to aid our daughter in sleeping through the train's annoying interruptions. We don't get to spend too much time at the retreat center because of excessive driving time between the retreat center and each church we were scheduled in (that's another story altogether), but the best thing is being here with friends, friends who are like family. That makes any situation more than livable!

———-

A sigh escapes my lips as we disembark from the car after several hours folded inside. Yay! An actual HOUSE, I think. We walk in the door of the cute little house, one block over from the church that owns it. It appears there is new flooring, recently painted walls, and...nothing else. A couch from decades past and a matching chair, mini blinds on the many windows, but no curtains. Every wall is bare. The refrigerator sits forlornly alone against the opposite wall facing the rest of the single-wall style kitchen, a little round table and three chairs gracing the middle of the kitchen area. Blessed space though, two bedrooms. Sure, there is only a bed in one of the rooms, but that's okay. Our daughter carries her own bed with her, so sharing space with some random unpacked boxes and renovation materials really is no trouble for her. Blocking out the light streaming through the windows, however, is another story. Good thing we have tacks with us at all times (they come in handy for covering sunny windows with whatever extra blankets might be on hand). My child's affinity for darkness when she sleeps has proven one of the only unchanging caveats requiring some real wit and invention in a few of the places we've stayed. Three days with nothing to do but read (yes, reading my Bible is a standard of my day, but spending 16 hours per day trying to focus on the holy Word of God when my two year old requires attention or direction is not even close to possible. Now, this house is cute, a good size, relatively clean (though the newly done floors could use a good Swiffer Wet cleaning, as they leave our feet black from whatever dirt residue clings to them). But, with no TV, no utensils or dishes for cooking (nope, not a single pot, pan, or casserole dish on site), what options can creative minds engender for making the best of slim amenities? Hmmm, necessity begins to mother invention when two year olds and long evening hours begin requesting Elmo movies. So, always the equipped missionaries, we do what any self-respecting, make lemonade with lemons kind of people do; we set up our projector in the empty living room and project our portable DVD player onto the bare wall. So, Elmo on the "big screen" can be quite entertaining, when his smile is bigger than my toddler's whole frame and his high-pitched voice seems to envelope the entire room. Oh yes, projecting DVD's is a huge success. Score one for missionary inventiveness. Several other Disney characters and fan favorites premiere on that blank wall in the following days, making the time fly. It even slightly makes up for the emergency vehicles literally screaming by the house multiple times throughout each day and night of our stay (thanks in part to the three block proximity of a hospital and fire station). As they say in real estate: Location, Location, Location. Ah, armed with only the inexplicable joy of a big screen, what we humans can survive!

———-

Have you ever had one of those dreams where you are stuck inexplicably at school, end up living in the nurse's station, sleeping on a teachers' lounge sofa, and sneaking food from the cafeteria kitchen in the middle of the night? Yeah, neither have I, but I imagine that some of the prophet's chambers we have stayed in might feel a little like that. Several churches also house Christian schools, amazing ministries that reach many needs in a community. Sleeping in a room off the school's main hallway like one of the classrooms gets a little awkward for a couple of reasons. First, all parents of infants and toddlers know that sleep time is precious and can be easily interrupted or stolen all together, and absence of precious sleep makes for an absence of a peaceful day as well. Second, one cannot quiet the inevitable noise of a kitchen only a wall away.

One such church/school offers a lovely prophet's chamber right beside the office of the school's principal, with classrooms on every other side down the remainder of the hallway. The chamber itself is very comfortable and pretty, simple and clean, and we are allowed to use the church's kitchen for cooking (the same facilities used by the students and teachers for lunch during the school day). The caveats: Kids streaming rambunctiously down the hallway at 7 in the morning. Teenage guffaws and excited chatter piercing the calm at structured intervals throughout the morning and afternoon. A purposefully loud "Outside for P.E." sounding down the corridor during a baby's tenuous hold on sleep in the early afternoon. An awkward walk past a group of teachers at their customary lunch table into and out of a kitchen normally used by church family rather than passing strangers. Blessed silence after the final class lets out at 3. Atmosphere is sometimes everything. Here, it's everything but relaxing.

A similar experience occurs in another prophet's chamber that sits with its door adjacent to a church school's main door, the primary thoroughfare for teachers and students alike at 7 am as well as 2:30 in the afternoon. Hard for a toddler to nap through loud calls for specific students every two minutes during the afternoon pick up rush. Failed naps and cranky toddlers are a small price to pay for a roof over our heads, but it doesn't make it any more pleasant. So much for that dream about sleeping in a school surrounded by books and quiet, raiding the cafeteria at midnight and glugging all the chocolate milk that you can get your hands on. In reality, it's a little more nightmare than fantasy.

———-

We often come across mission apartments that occasionally serve church members themselves who are, for whatever reason, in need of temporary housing. It's wonderful when churches are able to meet special needs like that which arise within their families. A room off the church gymnasium, a little nook kitchen (well, a sink, a fridge, and some cabinets), a three piece bath, and a bedroom just big enough for a queen bed. There is this giant floor TV. You know the ones...the ones from the 1970s and encased in wood so they are freakishly heavy and act as their own entertainment center. There is a dark green, stuffed fabric couch with cushions that are sinking in several places, making us wonder what adventures it's seen in days gone by. And the main corner of the apartment's living space is dominated by a dark wood bunk bed, one that has a double bed on the bottom with only a couple feet of space between the two bunks. Both beds are colorful, graced with mismatched sheets and thin blankets (no comforters) highlighting several different cartoon characters. Stains and crumbs hold tight to each blanket, in the same way dirt and spots seem regular ingredients of the kitchenette. I may be wrong, but I'm pretty sure that the fridge is growing things, and I'm not talking about legitimate science experiments. What's the first thought that goes through your mind when you open a utensil drawer in a kitchen and see something move into the corner? Yep, me too. Stepping back now! Let's just say that no cooking is happening in this space, nor will any resident utensils be used in the eating of our take out dinner. The same sentiments go for the shower; somehow allowing mildew and grime to overshadow every corner of a shower stall does not instill confidence in its clean-making abilities. Funny how that works. Blessedly, this is just a one night stay for us, but we are told a family of five in the church had stayed there for nearly six months prior to our stay. At least there is a Papa John's close by. Score!

——-

Driving along America's highways can be considered a botanist's dream, lush greenery as far as the eye can see, every type of tree, grass, and bush known to the American plains seen in sunlit glory. Okay so the cities often cut into the landscape, eradicating miles of beautiful plants for the sake of things as unimportant as, you know, people's homes and jobs and such. But, what's so intriguing about America's luxurious stretches of unaltered forestry are the fabulous things that one finds hidden in the woods, exciting things you'd never imagine. Think Hansel and Gretel. They found that awesome cottage of candy...oh wait, I guess the whole evil witch wanting to eat them kind of put a damper on the whole grand adventure aspect. Well, we've never found a house made of cookie dough (though my husband might actually consider that a dream come true), but finding one church was a little like being an early explorer. Thick trees for miles, the GPS directing down a barely visible, barely paved road into the forest. The curve of the road seems to disappear into a screen of emerald leaves, and we wonder if we are being sent in a wrong direction (as the GPS has been known to do a time or two). Up and over a hill, around another tight bend, and then it appears: A giant white, pillared building in a clearing and a large oval of gravel creating a driveway into and out of the church's entrance. The weathered reddish bricks and white 30 foot tall pillars stand in stark contrast to the sea of greenery surrounding it, yet the effect of the setting is extremely peaceful and soothing. Uninterrupted by the city, the church property didn't even seem to have a real parking lot, just a small gravel area directly in front of the church doors (not space for more than five cars or so). It gave the sense of almost a nature retreat rather than a church, but the property was beautiful, glowing late afternoon sunlight shining through the tree tops and casting hazy shadows on the ground, making us simply want to breathe in deeply and drink in the utter freshness of pure air. The inside of the enormous building was split into two levels, the floor level set up as a kind of dormitory (used by the church during in-house conferences and educational seminars) with a long hallway lined with bedrooms (the first of which serves as the main mission apartment when needed). The olive green bathtub is a particular selling feature of this space, and I always marvel at the colors that previous decades have used to adorn households in this country...because, trust me, we've seen them all. The wood paneling is also quite striking, but the room is clean and decently comfortable. The sheer size of the building is also pretty impressive, as it is a notable trek to get to the laundry room on the far end of the kitchen, which is on the far end of the fellowship hall, which is on the far end of the expansive foyer. Needless to say, we stick pretty much to our room while there, but we always enjoy our stay (other than the Pizza Hut debacle of 2013, but I'll get to that in another chapter). Few things are as beautiful as God's pure creation in the great outdoors, and we've had the pleasure of seeing much of His artistry. No, we didn't find a cottage of candy or cookie dough, but the church in the trees is pretty neat on its own!

—— —-

Deputation would be a different story all together without a toddler. The extra luggage required. The diapers and wipes. The endless stock of raisins and milk. Plus, a young child who physically requires a nap each day poses special challenges that many places are not designed to meet.

One church houses a mission apartment in an on-site duplex. A fairly comfortable, yet very small space. The second (much larger) side of the duplex serves as a parsonage for the church's current youth pastor and his family. We usually end up having to be the most creative in playpen placement, and here is no exception. The only open space is in the kitchen yet again, back in the corner, against the back door. Great, floor space that isn't directly within the TV's scope of light! Bad news, it is beside the back door to the youth pastor's place. I never knew people could consistently slam doors that way. I didn't realize that people are often oblivious to how much noise they make on a regular basis. Every afternoon without fail, our child falls asleep after much struggle; 30 minutes later...next door suddenly bursts into a den of activity like a dormant fire just waiting for one twirl of a stick to blaze again to heated glory. The back door slams multiple times as several people make their way up the back stairs, skillfully tromping on each stair with precision and thud. People laugh, and kids run around as a mom calls for them to get ready for a nap (to which the response seemingly is NOTHING) and then calls several more times for acquiescence that never seems forthcoming. Every day, at precisely 30 minutes into my child's nap, she is aroused into screaming distress over the avalanche of activity that wakes her from a less than peaceful slumber two feet from where she lays her head. Each day, we are thwarted in our attempts at a peaceful afternoon, and by week's end, fatigue and irritation are starting to seamlessly blend into one. Thankfully, that stay only lasted a short while, and we left there for quieter shores. Thankfully, I can relive the memory in silence.

———-

The first thing that jumps out to this mommy when we arrive at the church is a private children's playground right beside the Family Life Center in which we'll be staying. Oh my goodness, an outdoor play area right outside? What a HUGE bonus! This place is already quite promising. We'll be here about ten days, so I'm hoping that it will be comfortable at least. The pastor's wife/church secretary meets us at the door to let us in and show us around. We walk into a building that must have been a community rec center in another life. It's been taken over by the children and teen ministries of the church, the foyer decorated as a colorful construction zone announcing a "Kid Zone" for young students to enter on Sunday mornings. Orange traffic cones and lots of reflector tape create quite the entrance to an otherwise messy, utility style building. We walk through the full-size basketball court; the "prophet's palace," as they have it titled, is situated in a room off the gym itself (Can you hear the reverberating basketballs banging through the room already? Yep, we did too). The walls are painted concrete blocks. No pesky beaming sunlight at all hours, but no sound insulation either. The door into our room faces two bathrooms (one of which has a nice, huge shower and the other which will serve as our daughter's bedroom: Yes, I know...a bathroom for a bedroom? Really? Yes, we do what we have to do, and a separate space is always conducive to better sleep for everyone). The room has a fridge, a microwave, and the smallest sink I've ever seen. Not even a legitimate kitchenette, but at least there's a big screen TV and cable and a comfy foam mattress pad on the bed. Those are always great pluses. The biggest difficulty when staying in such a utility type building is the plethora of machine noises one hears constantly throughout the day and night, from the drinking fountain coolers starting and stopping to the strains of wind on each inch of metal roofing and the vibrations of plumbing that accompany multiple bathrooms. Thinking twice about flushing the toilet because the echoing noise will wake your toddler is always fun! So the sound issue, not so awesome, but I do have to say that this particular "palace" has some pretty magazine worthy décor. Apparently, the church member "in charge" of this prophet's palace is a lover of interior design and quite the amateur artist. There were painted murals and floral prints gracing all four walls, a dominant black and white color palette making the room look cool and clean while pops of dark chartreuse keep the room from completely losing its livable feel. Glass birds and black painted tree branches adorn the cubicle shelves serving as room dividers as well as various flower pots throughout the space. Paisley patterns seem to be the favorite, as an entire wall is stenciled with one print, and each blanket and rug depicts a different yet coordinated pattern. My favorite piece, however, is an awesome end table. Now, this I love and can see myself creating my own version for our future house that's being decorated in my mind as we travel throughout the country. Its construction is simple (three vintage suitcases stacked). Its design is customizable (the top case is covered in various pieces of colored contact paper that match the tri-color design of the entire room). The suitcases are fun, just antique enough to look unique without being that kind of aged that comes off as dirty and creepy. So what do I do? Take pictures of course! I want to remember how to make one for myself. I'm imagining walking through a dusty resale shop in Melbourne, stumbling upon a few awesome leather suitcases from the last century and creating my own original piece, at a steal of a price for sure! Okay, so I'm hoping that I can find cool and cheap ways to decorate any future abode we actually get to personalize, but until then I'm collecting ideas, and this room (though WAY too floral and fluffy for real life- and certainly too much for my husband- and not really great for long term living with loud noises and no stove) provides several great tips and tricks for inexpensive decorating.

———-

We have stayed in plenty of rooms that are within or attached to a church's private school. This room, however, takes the cake. We are told to arrive before the end of the school day, so that someone will be there to let us in. We arrive in the early afternoon and are met with only locked doors. It takes several minutes before anyone inside even notices the random guy walking around knocking on doors and looking inside the few visible windows. Finally, the side door opens, and the pastor's wife introduces herself. We are ushered inside and are told that "there are plenty of boys who aren't doing anything and can help carry your things upstairs if you need them to." I find it interesting that all these kids are at school yet supposedly doing nothing, but we simply decline the offer and follow her up the stairs. With each step, a realization begins. The floors are creaking and squeaking and generally making a lot of noise. I move to one side of the hallway; the floors creak. I move to the other side; the floors squeak. I have never experienced floors quite so determined to make themselves known. Throughout our week-long stay, we discover only a couple of silent spots in the entire area we have to occupy. The bathroom floor is actually the worst. Have you ever stood so still that you realize you're actually moving, like being in a skyscraper and realizing the wind is blowing the entire building around? Generally, we aren't quiet enough or still enough to notice when we change position slightly or gently sway as we redistribute weight from one foot to another. But trust me, we move more than you'd think. I have the experience of this bathroom to prove it. I brush my teeth, and the whirring of my electric toothbrush is nearly silenced by the symphony of sound coming from the weak, laminate floor. I literally stand as still as I can, just to see if the floor will fall silent. In my attempt to listen to the floor, I am apparently doing a jig while standing still because the creaking never stops. It seems as though even nodding my head causes the floor to emit a screeching response. The rest of the room is pleasant enough, clean and usable. The bed is one of the least comfortable we have ever experienced, but at least we have next to no noise issues with the school below. That is a tremendous blessing. Thankfully, our daughter's naps aren't disturbed by recess time, but I certainly don't spend her naps walking around much on that floor. It's an interesting thing when floorboards make more noise than a building full of students. Just be aware how much noise you really make when you're standing still. I bet you'll be surprised! I know I was.

———-

Perfectly manicured lawns. Two-story buildings covered in pristine glass and brand new brick. A seemingly new duplex house sitting in the church's front parking lot, unassuming in its quiet, tidy repose. One door labeled "Mission House" and the other stating simply "Mission Apt." Ah, a nice, newer place, which usually always means clean. Cleanliness! With cable even! A four hour drive now over, I am excited to get to our destination and find it such a pleasant sight to behold, a promising start. The apartment side in which we're staying has two bedrooms, two bathrooms, and a nice size living area. Beds are new yet not comfortable in the least (a common feature of mission apartments-really uncomfortable beds), and the heater/air conditioner has to be "worked on" more times than it worked in the week we're here. But, the thing that strikes me within seconds of entering the front door: the non-existent kitchen. If you've ever spent an extended period of time in a hotel room with only a mini fridge and a microwave, you may have some idea what using this "kitchenette" (and I use the term very loosely) is like. Room for only a few cans of soda, a gallon of milk, and a few small bottles of water in the fridge. No freezer, no ice, zero counter space (thanks to a lovely Keurig coffee maker), and one tiny sink. This lovely "home" provides no way to cook or store fresh food. Well, that'll make the week's meals more fun. The voice in my head is not amused by my sarcasm, but it could be worse. Hmmm, we can't even buy frozen meals to make in the microwave because there's no freezer to keep it in. Right next door (attached to the side) is the "Mission House" fully stocked with a full kitchen, a stove and a regular refrigerator. No one is staying next door, so we think, "Hmmm, maybe we could just put some frozen stuff in that freezer until we need it or possibly cook dinner on the stove in the evenings if no one is using it." It seems like a perfectly rational, easy solution to the dilemma of needing to go out for each meal. A quick text to the associate pastor, however, threw another wave into the already troubled waters of our current living arrangements: No, he said, you can't use the stove OR the fridge; we sometimes have staff meetings over there, and...yeah, we just don't want you to use it. What??? Now, this makes absolutely no sense! A perfectly good and unused fridge and stove sit directly on the other side of the laundry room door in an otherwise completely empty house, and we can't access them for a single meal because the church may hold staff meetings in the mission house? What??? Yeah, we didn't get it either. Weird. My response, as one might imagine, is to roll my eyes in frustration, feeling akin to an adolescent being banished to the toddlers' table for Thanksgiving dinner. Really, that's how it's going to be? We see how we rate, and it isn't much higher, apparently, than the proverbial red-headed stepchild. Yeah, that is what this deputation thing feels like sometimes, but we've definitely had worse. Really, this simply proves an even bigger reality of deputation and the Christian life in general: Attitude is just about everything (on the giving and receiving end). People who offer a welcoming spirit of love and Christian fellowship make even the most mediocre accommodations seem cozy, and the most palatial space feels cold and unpleasant when accompanied by derision and patronizing on the part of the host. Thankfully, we were allowed to use the shared laundry room. Awesome! A potty-training toddler requires extra clothing changes, as we've quickly learned.

Funny thing, we never did see or hear a single person using the adjacent mission house even once during our stay. Well, I'm glad we left it alone for them anyhow. Who knows what might've happened!

———-

It is a beautiful space. Brand new appliances, fresh paint, pristine furniture, modern decorations, and matching linens. Plus, boasting more square footage than our parents' homes. It is a gorgeous, new mission apartment in a gigantic space, left over and converted from one church ministry into another. I am always amazed by the difference that can be made with relatively few things: clean, unified décor, newer appliances. These are the stuff that dream homes are made of. My husband likes the mega big screen in the living room, while I gleefully consider the possibilities with a new dishwasher, clean bathtubs, and plush, squishy bath mats. Guys. They say that women are impractical. However, I have yet to see my husband value the laundry and cooking faculties over the availability of cable TV and internet. What we notice, however, the first day in this beautiful space is the utter lack of windows. There are none. Nada. Zero. Zilch. The building originally had long, narrow windows that spanned floor to ceiling at six feet intervals around the outer walls, but for (presumably) the sake of simple insulation and dry wall, they are all covered over, leaving the space with absolutely no natural light. See our bodies run on this sleep/ wake system that is largely synced with the light of day and the darkness of night. God made it pretty natural like that. You always think how totally weird it would be to live in one of those faraway places (you know...like Alaska) where they have continuous light for half the year and non-stop dark for the other six months. People have existed in such circumstances for millennia, but I'm sure that it is not an easy thing to become accustomed to. Consequently, we learn quite quickly how much total darkness can induce lethargy. The incredible upside is the ease with which our toddler naps and sleeps long, long, long hours as there is no irritating sunlight to disturb her. The downside is that all of us end up sleeping much more than normal as we aren't accustomed to waking with no beaming herald of the morning peeking through the bedroom curtains. So, we make sure to get our daily allotment of vitamin D playing at a local park and continue to enjoy the lovely space, my husband enthused by Sports Center on the big screen and me thoroughly taking advantage of the resident dishwasher. Though God designed us to function optimally in conjunction with the sunlight (and we do miss it at times-like at 9 am when we are just realizing it's morning), we really enjoy that space. You can never discount the power of the fluffy bath mats, after all.

———-

We pull into the church's driveway or rather the grassy knoll that seems to sit outside the church doors (there isn't actually any designated parking space). The pastor said there was a mission apartment in a building behind the church. Hmmm, we see several structures, none of which are marked and only one of which looks even big enough to house...anything. The pastor lives next door, and the adjacent mobile home provides quite a welcome with its lawn cluttered by a plethora of metal objects and unused "junk" for lack of any other functionally descriptive term. The trees and lawn are overgrown; leaves, grass, and vegetation hang heavily against the roof and front porch, decorating the moss-covered shingles on the house as well as the innumerable, rusty inhabitants of the yard. My daughter sneezes, a sure sign that the allergies in the late winter air are in full bloom amongst all these trees and shrubberies. After circling around the block and back into the church property, we finally see a man, who we presume to be the pastor, come outside and open a large swinging gate behind the mobile home that leads to another acre of land, mostly empty but for a small building in the far corner. He motions for us to drive back to the small building, where we are finally able to get out of the car. After introducing himself, he leads us into the building that houses their "mission apartment." I wonder if the church actually uses this building currently, as there is a room designated as a Sunday school room and a nursery room. A round weather-beaten table, surrounded by mismatched metal and wooden chairs, sits in the center of what can only be described as the house's original living area, now presumably serving as a meeting space of some kind. Though we are still not clear on the last time the space was actually used. The walls are a tan color and blend in seamlessly with the dingy, ratted carpeting. Apparently this building houses no vacuums because the floors seem to sigh dust and dirt and other elements right into the air as we step upon them. This, however, is only the beginning of this adventure. The living area is bordered by a small kitchen, the kind with dark wood cupboards and colored appliances. I spy that tell-tale "dirt" (at least that's a word we'd use for it on the field-you know the kind I'm talking about) along the countertops, left by whatever critters must indeed be living there. The ancient stove top set into the countertop is covered in rust and old greasy grime. The sink is chalky with paint stains, and the only "cleaning instrument" present is a rusty looking metal sponge resembling a burnt biscuit. Yes sadly, three unsuspecting bugs had come to their ends on that countertop, their tiny bodies lying desolate and forgotten and stiff. The pastor now informs us about the church's food pantry, fondly relating the wonderful ministry provided to their community. This house contains the extra storage of supplies donated to the food pantry, and we are welcome to eat whatever we'd like (except the 100+ cartons of orange juice in the fridge, as they are way past their date and haven't been thrown out yet). The freezer, the contents of which he graciously offers, is filled to capacity by unidentifiable packages of meat in various sizes and colors. As I'm trying not to touch anything, we are ushered through the original back door onto an additional porch/room space that is full of various machines and wood and metal and very cramped. A makeshift double door, fashioned to fit the space by sawing off parts of two larger doors, opens into the mission room. Picture a double bed lined by a tall dresser along one side and a rollaway bed on the other side (this is the width of the room). Approximately 12 inches from the foot of the bed stands another tall chest of drawers spanning the wall between the end of the bed and the door, the other wall space filled by a single chair and two random cardboard boxes (this is the length of the room). There is about three square feet of floor space, and we climb onto the bed from its foot. The walls inside the room have been recently painted a simple, clean taupe but are overshadowed by unfinished floors, improvised doors, and dusty, broken furniture. I feel the walls closing in around me, my breath getting stifled in the stale air. Shortly, we are alone, left to unpack the few things we'll need for overnight. It's still early afternoon. What to do? Taking advantage of available features, I take my daughter into the nursery room to play (a great way to kill some time). She quickly finds some trucks and stuffed animals to play with, but my ease is short-lived. I spot another two dead but unwanted friends hanging out morosely in the middle of the nursery floor, inches from where my daughter is playing, and the changing table sports another fun assortment of "dirt" and debris from what I'll never know. This just will not work. We certainly cannot spend the evening in this atmosphere wiling away several more hours until bedtime. I sense a crack beginning in my resolve to appreciate everything, so we do the best, cheapest thing we know: We find a shopping mall and spend our evening out of that building, strolling through Barnes and Noble, having dinner, and only returning in time to turn in for the night (making sure our daughter's bed is not touching a wall in case things are lurking around in the night: I have yet to find visitors in her bed while on the road, and I won't start now). We are up early that next morning, no alarm needed. At least repacking the car only takes a couple minutes since we don't have much inside. That's always nice!

———-

The ceilings are at least 15 feet. The lights are commercial grade and fluorescent bright. The windows are floor to ceiling. The room design mimics a hotel suite, with two double beds, a small dinette set, a desk, a set of comfy arm chairs creating a seating area, a spotless bathroom back in the corner, and a kitchenette along the far wall. The walls are decorated sparingly but cohesively with several printed Bible verses and a couple pieces of religious artwork. One of my favorites is that of a man who is clearly wounded and hurting from the world's presence, a dark devilish shadow rises menacingly behind his shoulder, but the man's Savior stands right behind him, holding the weary man up in His arms and keeping him from falling prey to the roaring lion awaiting. Every time I've seen it, I am reminded that no matter how close Satan gets (and he gets really close sometimes), our Savior is always closer, for Christ hold His children in His arms where they can never be let go. This particular apartment has seen us many times throughout our deputation travels. The room is within the church building, situated beside the church's kitchen with a separate entrance on the side of the building. Now, we love this church and have many great memories in this particular room (like when our 6 month old baby tried solid food for the first time, dribbling rice cereal all over her face, and when she decided it would be funny at 9 months old to bump her head against the wall then smile and say "Owie" before doing it again). The only caveat to a fully relaxing stay, however, is a signal security system. Whenever any outside door throughout the entire, large church building is opened or closed, a shrill, shrieking ding-dong style bell sounds. There is a speaker right outside the apt door (understandably on the main door into the church's kitchen). You've heard those home systems that meter out a staccato beep, beep, beep when the front or back doors are opened. They alert the household when someone or something is moving. They sound relatively innocuous until a mischievous child starts opening and closing doors on purpose, turning a simple alert into a slow dripping of torturous tones on the auditory nerves, your brain silently crying for relief from the assault. I've always found those beep systems to be purposeful yet so incredibly annoying that I could never want one in my own home. Anyway, this church has such a system; except theirs is not just a repetition of simple monotone beeps. Theirs sounds like quick nails scraping a chalkboard, two beats of discordant sounds that scratch the ear and leave it raw. If there was a way to quiet or silence the signal within the mission apartment itself, the relaxation factor would triple. Yet when our daughter naps during the day, I outwardly cringe every time the signal sounds, listening intently for the telltale whimpers of a baby disturbed out of sleep. Her being woken from her nap happens more than once, especially when there is something going on at the church where people are streaming in and out. Mission apartments are definitely a tremendous blessing to us; commercial spaces simply pose some interesting challenges to calm living. That's okay though. It can always be worse. Being around great people is certainly worth a little abuse to our ears!

———-

So, the gamut of living quarters and conditions certainly exists within the world of missionary accommodations. And the gamut certainly includes those we consider true sanctuaries (those places that make us feel like we are in a home, not just a space). One major element to a home is the ability to make memories (especially with those you love), and we have found some places are favored because they afford us the option of dining at an actual table and/or having friends or family over for fellowship. We loved hosting meals when we had our own apartment, and that's definitely something that we miss being out on the road full-time.

One of the best mission houses in which we've had the privilege to stay is a perfect example of this. We've gotten to stay in this particular home on several occasions, and we have made a lot of fun memories there. A major perk is having a lovely dining space and being able to invite people over. Homemade Texas chili simmering invitingly on the stove. Cornbread muffins hot out of the oven, sweet buttery goodness wafting into the air. Brownies cooling on the counter. The table is set with matching plates and bowls, folded paper towels for napkins, and glasses fogging with the chill of ice beginning to melt in the room temperature. A call to dinner and a parade of feet gathering in a space set aside for just this moment, a collection of familiar faces bound by love and blood and of course...a common hunger at dinnertime. As the large stainless steel pot of chili is placed in the center of the laden table, a chorus of "ooh, yum..." sounds simultaneously from each chair. The family joins hands and bows to give thanks for the One who provided as well as the provision. As amen is repeated by each member present, muffins are passed, green beans are dished out, and chili is ladled carefully into waiting bowls. I've learned how much we take for granted about the simple act of getting together with those we love, spending time sharing food, love, and life with each other, and this particular house (in addition to having all the wonderful, comfy amenities that one could wish for) has provided us with many more such memories of excitement (our daughter took her first steps in that living room) of fellowship (I actually got to cook many times for people there, and we celebrated our daughter's second birthday with our friends there), memories that we will treasure always. The Wi-Fi and cable TV, laundry and full kitchen, the beautiful master bedroom suite, and the fluffy matching towels are fantastic! We are always incredibly thankful when we are blessed to stay in a place that's clearly taken care of and a real gift of love from a church. But, it's the ability to share our life with others, the ability to see a friend's eyes light up when she recognizes the chewy, chocolaty yumminess she will enjoy with one of my famous brownies, the childhood milestones experienced, and the love that we get to experience there that brilliantly illuminate a meaningful life. Those moments are what make that particular house a favorite. That is what makes any house into a home even if you don't get to stay very long!

———-

Detailing every church, house, and room we've stayed in would probably cure any insomniac, but rather than bore with repetitive detail, I will simply point out that we have been in countless cities, in countless rooms (whether in a person's home or in the church offices), in countless beds. We've certainly on occasion been able to enjoy such amenities as big screen tvs, OnDemand cable, and fast Wi-Fi internet. We've stayed in houses of all sizes; one had five bedrooms. We've stayed in hotel rooms, and people's basements. We've stayed in dorm rooms and Sunday school rooms. Our daughter's slept in bathrooms and hallways, kitchens and living rooms. I think I've experimented with six or seven different pillows, searching for the greatest level of comfort and still not quite achieving it. It's a unique predicament, living in so many different types and styles of "homes." We'll never be totally comfortable here. We'll never be exactly at home here. But, we feel even more prepared for the foreign field, where apartments might not be what we expect, where amenities might not be all we hoped for, where our daughter's room may barely be the size of a small office, where central AC doesn't exist and kitchen space is hard to find. Every mission apartment, mission house, prophet's chamber, and private room that was generously opened to us during our travels has blessed us. God has enabled us to experience more in the past three years than most experience in entire lifetimes, adjusting, being content, and making it work, whatever the IT may happen to be. We've built quite a vision in our minds of our home on a foreign land, the one we will live in some day. No place is perfect, but I'm pretty sure that anything we can call our own and make our own will be as close as we'll ever need.

Chapter Four: These are the Voyages of the U.S.S. Sorrento

To say that deputation is an adventure is a tremendous understatement. Many movies have been made to depict the crazy, unexpected, and emotional happenings of families and friends on vacations and road trips. To be on the road for a short vacation usually provides memorable fodder for inside jokes and sibling bonds that exist forever. To live on the road full-time is to be in a constant state of movement and uncertainty, a state in which anything can happen on the turn of a dime. Throughout the time we've spent traveling the country, we have collected more random experiences than can really be relayed in a single volume of stories, but through it all, we have learned one thing above all: Our God is the same yesterday, today, and forever. No matter where we are, what time zone we are in, whether those around us are friend or foe, we have discovered the immutable grace and love of our Savior and Lord who calls us and sustains us in everything. I wish that I could remember every single detail, every moment that made us laugh out loud or roll our eyes, each tear that was shed and each lonely sigh that was felt to the depths of our soul, each magnificent display of God's creation and artistry that has taken our breath completely away. But, suffice it to say that deputation is a journey. It is an adventure. It is a whirlwind and a desert. It is a grind and a vacation. It is a struggle and a joy. It is a difficulty and a breeze. It is utter dependence on the One who is Ruler of all. It is finishing each day with the knowledge that we know nothing and He knows everything. It is an emptying of self to make way for His plan, a plan so full of blessings it blows my mind and a plan so uniquely reliant on Him that the days of disappointment in humanity can sometimes feel suffocating. It is deputation. It is JUST THE BEGINNING!

———-

There are few things as fun or as exhausting as back to back missions conferences. With a six week old baby and a borrowed van, we set out on the greatest whirlwind trip of our deputation "career". 40 days. 5 missions conferences. Ohio, Iowa, Michigan, Georgia, and Texas. Non-stop. Every day is packed with activity and services and/or driving to the next state and destination. Though those days are a bit of blur now, I remember being so excited to be in each place, meeting so many new people, showing off a new baby (which always gets plenty of attention in a Baptist church), feeling overwhelmed by the welcome and love of the people. We are taken to many museums and other amusements throughout that month as each church wants us to enjoy the highlights of their city and feel cared for. We share many wonderful meals and laughing fellowship and thoroughly enjoy each family of believers. Each conference ends, we pack everything up once again and drive non-stop to the next place where another conference is starting the very next day. When we return to TX and our apartment (which we still had at the time), we realize just how taxing the trip has been, but we feel so fully blessed to have been a part of each and every moment. Our six week old is now officially a missionary on deputation, and throughout these first crazy weeks, she's been fully acquainted with what traveling and deputation includes. I don't remember all the hours in the car, but each and every church is a lovely part of our reminiscence and now our mission family. That's a blessing that makes all the fatigue just a distant memory.

———-

Small town America is specifically non-descript. I know that sounds like an oxymoron, but there are some features of small American towns that are so uniquely American yet so universal that a person really could be anywhere. Downtown squares and tree-lined streets. Kids' bicycles and laundry lines. A fun thing to discover when traveling this country is the local festivals that seem to be the pride of each of these small towns. They all have them, an excuse for carnival rides and fried foods on sticks and local talent competitions. One such city in OH in which we stay hosts a popcorn festival each year. It's a huge town celebration, complete with parade and rides and booths from every city group and organization. The mission apartment we are staying in is just a couple blocks from downtown where this festival is set up, so it's a simple matter of pulling out the stroller for our infant in order to experience the merriment. We decide to splurge a bit and try fried Oreos for the first time (tasty, but a bit too mushy for our palettes). One interesting tidbit, the popcorn festival is actually quite void of popcorn. We walk the whole carnival and find only two booths that are even selling popcorn. Interesting. But, the local businesses sure turn out to spread their names and get some marketing in. Every church is represented as well, many passing out tracts and invitations to services. We are also told to keep an eye out for the Gay Alliance Church that usually has a booth fairly close to the Baptist church's. A person really can't miss the large rainbows decorating their space (an always slightly disheartening use of God's beautiful promise). My husband, realizing that this will be an issue for which we need an answer no matter where we go, picks up their pamphlet "God vs. Gays," a nonsensically laughable read if fiction, tragic as a real piece of propaganda, misguided by misinterpreted scripture and a clear desire to justify rather than be redeemed from sin. We certainly cannot forget that city, that festival, that "church" or the lessons that we learn there. No matter the beauty or seeming perfection of a city, there is within humanity always the sin nature and darkness that only God can quell. It is His truth and His light that must shine to every corner of this world so that people may be saved. Even in small town America, people must daily fight against the influence of the devil among them. This is why we must go where God sends us; for surely, there is need everywhere for His light.

———-

So we're from Texas where the meat of choice is pure beef, many people jokingly considering anything less to be simply fare for wimps. With more industry than beach on our coasts, seafood is not a large part of Texan culture. Florida, on the other hand, is all about its seafood. The fish fry is such a large part of people's gatherings there that the accomplished fry cook is held in esteem equal to that of the best "grillers" in the lone star state. We have experienced a few different fish fry events during our visits to Florida, but one stands out above the rest.

One family in a south Florida church with which we are staying invites us over for a home cooked meal. Home cooking while traveling, as I've mentioned before, is always a welcome treat. But when you do not know the cooks, you can often feel awkward about going to a person's home, sitting at their kitchen table, and sometimes eating things you've never seen before. We follow the couple's car through a maze of streets lined thickly by greenery, making us feel like we are nearing the Everglades. Upon entering their mobile home, we find a larger group than expected over for what is apparently a regular scheduled fish fry in their home. We are told by everyone there that "we haven't had real fish fry" until we have tried theirs. So, we fellowship around the living area until dinner is called. We all sit in mismatched chairs around a large, high, round table in the middle of the open kitchen area. It is here that we first learn about and taste the Florida delicacy of rice topped with tomatoes. Though we aren't used to the classically southern soul food of collard greens and black eyed peas, the meal is in fact excellent, the fried fish perfectly seasoned and cooked (proof positive of the rave reviews we've been hearing all evening). It is a fun evening of laughter and fellowship with brothers and sisters in Christ that will prove to be a very rare occasion during deputation. We will always appreciate the time that this gracious family took to invite us over and share their home and cooking skills with us for that evening. It brightened our lives and our taste buds.

———

Sunday mornings are always busy, and when we are going to a brand new church for a Sunday morning service, we truly never know what we will encounter. Florida has provided several interesting beginnings for our Sundays. One such meeting is scheduled to be at a church that is just outside a Native American reservation in south Florida. That morning, we've driven through miles and miles of endless sugar cane fields and groves of orange trees, able to count on one hand the number of buildings we've seen. We begin to wonder if the GPS is accurately directing us, and then we see it. Right on the edge of a field is a small clearing with palm trees dotting the lawn. The GPS leads us to the clearing, and we discover the church hidden among the fields of sugar cane. But, it isn't the church itself that surprises us when we pull in. It is such a quiet and serene morning; we never would've guessed what we are to find. Flashing emergency lights meet us in the parking lot. An ambulance with its back door open and no siren (thankfully) sits in front of the church's main door, taking up several parking spaces. We do not see anyone outside, so we park and simply sit in our vehicle for several minutes. We begin to pray for the situation even though we have no clue what is going on. Seconds tick by, I have no idea how many. Finally, two EMT's emerge, wheeling out a man on a stretcher. My husband and I look at each other as we wonder what to do. When the ambulance is gone, we get out of the car and wonder if anyone else is around the silent property. Within a few minutes, a woman, introducing herself as the pastor's wife, exits the church building and meets us. The pastor has been taken to the hospital with severe kidney stones and will not be present for church. Hmm, no pastor. Okay, no worries. My husband can lead Sunday school and the regular service as well. The pastor's wife informs us that only one older gentleman will be in attendance for the first service. This may be a little strange. It's always difficult to "preach" to a group of one. The services go as smoothly as possible, though the people are largely silent, even during the handshaking time. When the services come to a close, several people kindly thank us for being there and smile warmly, which certainly helps make things less uncomfortable. The pastor's wife takes us out for lunch at a local place featuring yummy local dishes (I try the Indian taco-which is really delicious) in a lush setting of green trees and sprawling fields of sugar cane. This meeting is memorable, not because of a new soul stirring sermon or an ornate building, but we will always remember this meeting because of the reminder from God that we are to be prepared to serve in any way that He needs at a second's notice. Sometimes He simply wants us to be present and prepared, able to do whatever may be needed. We are not sure why God didn't allow us to meet that pastor in person, but we pray that we were able to minister and be a blessing to those people in his absence.

———-

South Carolina is a beautiful state. Historical Charleston. Lovely beaches. Gorgeous trees and cobblestone streets all around. We are going to spend the day exploring. We start the car like every other morning. My husband puts the Kia in gear, and the engine seems to be sputtering and jerking oddly. What?! Okay, maybe it's just a bit cold and needs to warm up some. So, we drive out of the parking lot. Now, our vehicle is only about six months old at this point. What in the world is going on? The lights on the dash begin flashing; the "service engine soon" symbol starts blinking rapidly. This is NOT a good thing! Um, we need to stop the car, IMMEDIATELY! What do we see up ahead? A Ford dealership. Well, that's better than nothing, so we pull into the service center and cut the engine, breathing a sigh of relief that we haven't left engine parts trailing behind us. A uniformed tech meets us outside and asks how to help. A short conversation later: a Kia dealership must be called. They can't really do anything for us there relating to warranty work. Oooh-kay. So, what to do now? Ah. The 1-800 Kia roadside assistance number. Yes! We knew that buying a new car was a good idea! So, we call; they send a tow truck. 2 hours later...we are headed toward a Kia dealership, my husband riding in our SUV on top of the tow truck bed while I and my infant and her car seat sit up in the truck's cab with the driver. This is as fun as you can imagine and not quite the exploring we'd planned for the day. Thankfully, people in South Carolina are quite friendly; southern charm is a real thing after all. Within a few minutes of arriving and getting settled in the red vinyl waiting room chairs at the Kia dealership, we are herded back outside by a tech who "knows exactly what the problem is." A mouse. Say what? He points to a space on the engine where he saw a mouse scurry out as soon as the hood was opened. But, it isn't simply the rodent presence that has caused our car trouble. Hungry mice munch. Hungry mice munch many wires. Ugh! Seriously? Oh yes, the fuel injection wires were apparently particularly scrumptious that prior evening. He'd chewed through a couple of them. And you guessed it...manufacturer's warranty doesn't cover the opening of a Kia rodent buffet. $250 later, we have learned a very important lesson: People in South Carolina are really nice. South Carolina mice? Not so much! And whatever you do...don't park on the grass.

———-

Colorado is full of sweeping vistas and lovely views. And there is often a LOT of space between towns. But when you stay overnight in a random place, 20 miles off the highway, you don't always know what you will experience.

It's late afternoon, and the sun is going down. We've been driving all day long, and our baby is really ready to be out of the car. Toys are being systematically thrown all over the backseat as their entertainment factor is now completely depleted. After exiting the interstate and driving a seemingly endless road through fields, we come upon a little Colorado town, hidden away amidst vast farmland. We find the church which will be our hotel for the evening and are met by a friendly couple from the church. We are let into the church's fellowship hall and discover a homey, decorated little bedroom not much larger than the double bed inside it. There is a plate of homemade cookies sitting like a welcoming hug on the kitchen counter with a note from the pastor's wife. She'd even bought us a frozen pizza for dinner. Wow! We were appreciative and hungry and feeling blessed. Fast forward a few hours. It's after 10:30 pm. The baby has been sleeping over an hour already, peacefully lying in her pack 'n play in the fellowship hall amongst the tables and folding chairs. My husband and I are hanging out in the bedroom, watching a news show when the phone starts to ring...loudly! We feel like ninjas as we creep out into the dark hall in order to reach the phone in the kitchen. It rings three times before we make it across the floor. Ringer OFF. Holding our breath, listening for baby. No sound. Baby's still sleeping soundly. Whew! Gracious, who would be calling the church this late at night? We have no idea, but the caller attempts two more times. It isn't our phone; we certainly are not answering it. As we tiptoe back into the bedroom, it seems as though the caller has finally given up, and we breathe a sigh of relief. Crisis averted. Just as we get settled back onto the bed a few minutes later, a crash sounds outside our door. Suddenly we see light flood underneath our door and a sense of dread overtakes us. Oh no! As we pull open the bedroom door, our startled and now awake daughter begins to wail. I rush over to get her as a man stares at us from the doorway of the fellowship hall. Who are you? he demands. What are you doing here? Who let you in here? I was not informed that anyone was staying here this evening! I'm thinking: Seriously? My husband informs the intruder who we are and who unlocked the door and let us in. I'm starting to get the baby calmed down and try to hint that our child was sleeping and needs to get back to it. The tornado who crashed into the church finally seems to get the point that we are there "legally," though he's clearly still hung up on the idea that "no one told him" that anyone would be there. After a few more minutes, the man ultimately decides to bid us good night and leaves as brusquely as he appeared without so much as a by your leave or a genuine apology for terrifying our baby in the middle of the night. Wow! We didn't expect that. We were very thankful for the pastor's wife's welcome and hospitality, but we were excited to be on our way the next morning.

———-

When you travel full-time, you stop at a lot of gas stations. When you visit a lot of gas stations, the times you encounter people asking for money goes up quite a bit. It is always interesting the way that people will approach perfect strangers and ask for money. Sadly, giving money to people who beg for it does not generally end well. For the most part, we have found it isn't prudent to supply monetarily a person who simply pounces on random strangers. But, there have been times when it seemed like a good idea. One such time sticks out in my mind. We pull into a Chevron for a quick fill up; we have another five or six hours to drive that day, so we are not lazing around. The baby needs a change, so as my husband takes care of the car, I have created a makeshift changing station on the back seat of the SUV. My child is unclothed; she's wriggling around. I'm trying to get a new diaper correctly placed when a guy and a child in a pickup interrupt my progress. He pulls up beside our car and asks if I can spare some cash. He concocts a story about needing gas money to get home for a nondescript reason. The child is looking up at me expectantly, and I'm trying not to look irritated as I attempt to listen while keeping a baby from rolling off the seat in nothing but a wet wipe. Really? You're asking me this now? My mind is trying to weigh the situation, but truthfully, I just want to be rid of them in order to complete the more important task of taking care of my own child. What would Jesus do? Okay, so I didn't really ask myself that in that moment, but I figured I would give them the benefit of the serious doubt in the forefront of my mind. I had two dollar bills within reach, so I grabbed them and handed them to the man, while the child looks sadly at me. At this point, I'm just wanting to finish my own parenting job, so I tell the man that I hope it helps. As I return to the baby in the car, the pickup truck disappears, out of the parking lot, gone from sight and my life forever. There is no indication that he needed that money for an emergency gallon of gas as he claimed. There is no indication that he was anything but an opportunist who took advantage of my busy, distracted moment to beg some cash (using an innocent child as a way to inflict guilt upon his targets). Who knows? Maybe he was an angel unawares just checking to see how I'd respond in that moment. Either way, I have never forgotten that experience and always find myself wondering what really is the "right" way to handle those types of requests. I guess God can keep on teaching us His methods for loving people, and I will just leave the rest up to Him.

———

Getting regular mail or just mail order products while on full-time deputation is always an interesting dilemma. My husband and I most often have things sent to our parents' homes for pick up at a later time. But, it can be quite a game of logistics if you need something while in a random place. Two main examples come instantly to mind. One

November, both my mom and my aunt were trying to get birthday cards to me while we were staying at a church in far west Texas. We faithfully checked the church's mail box every day waiting on the promised correspondence. We let the pastor know that we were expecting items, but it took longer than we thought for them to arrive. It does feel a little funny checking the church's mail and then putting everything back in their box when none of it is for us, but I do eventually get the cards and thoroughly enjoy them. Next, we are in Arizona for a month, and we're running out of prayer cards. Now, no missionary worth his salt will be caught dead without some prayer cards. Insert wink here. What to do? Call for back up. A couple emails to my mother in law later, I have the promise of more cards coming in the mail. The only question is that we aren't really sure where the mail will actually go. The mailing address that we have for the church is not the physical address. The church mail, we learn, goes to the house of the church's maintenance man. Ah. No worries. Whenever it arrives, he'll just bring it to church with him where we can retrieve it. Problem solved. Issue resolved. But, there is one thing that has been a huge blessing to us while on the road, one thing that has enabled us to purchase various things online and be able to pick them up wherever we may be staying. If you've never done it, you are totally missing out! I'm talking about Wal-Mart's site to store, people. Wal-Mart online will ship your order to any Wal-Mart store in the country where you can pick it up...for FREE! No shipping. Free. It's awesome, and we've taken advantage of that more than once. Yes, getting mail on the road can be a logistical puzzle, but it's fun getting letters or items however they wind up in your hands.

———-

It's a rainy week in north Florida. Every day in fact, the rain pours down all afternoon, each afternoon. The fun thing about the church that we are staying in is their alarm system. We get strong warnings about the security system, which is set up basically right outside the door of the mission apartment. After a certain time each evening, we basically cannot step into any other part of the church building. Motion sensors will alert their security company immediately of any odd activity. We then find it humorous that the first thing we are complimented on by church staff is the fact that we successfully avoid setting off the alarm. Apparently, many other occupants aren't so conscientious.

Besides remembering the ever present alarm system, we also discover during our stay the many local events hosted by this particular church. The apartment is situated in a loft type space over the kitchen/fellowship hall. It's around 5:30 am. Why are we awake already? What is all that noise? Voices. Laughter. Chairs being dragged along the floor. We hear several tables being set up and moved just below us. What is going on? My husband slips from the bed to glance through the mini blinds on the window. The reason for our early morning wake-up call? The church is a registered voting location. It's time for local elections. As most people know, voting locales open early and stay open late. The volunteers manning the voting booths are clearly having a grand old time if their robust guffaws reverberating throughout the building are any indication. Fortunately as the actual voting gets underway, the noise does die down. By that point, we've been up for a couple of hours though. We are certainly adaptable to anything, and it truly isn't a hardship to work around a church's unique schedule. It is nice, however, to know ahead of time when large scale activities may take place beneath the bedroom. Oh well. It's certainly a memory that won't be erased, and it certainly brings a smile rather than a grimace; that's always a plus.

———-

Has a person's behavior ever seemed so ludicrous that it's hard to even take it seriously? My daughter and I are at a local mall. It's right around 10 am on a weekday. I park outside Dillard's and have approximately eight other cars in the entire mall parking lot with me. If memory serves, I'm in maybe the second space of a completely empty row, about three rows from the main doors. I get out and open my daughter's door. She's discarded her shoes yet again, a favorite past time for my toddler, so I stand at her door retrieving her shoes and replacing them before I can get her out of her car seat and out of the car (both the driver's side door and the back door are open). What happens next still boggles my mind. As I'm trying to find my child's shoes in the back seat, a large green pickup truck stops perpendicular to my SUV. The driver, a woman, begins honking loudly at me and waving her hand toward the space next to my car (space #3 in the otherwise empty row). I'm still trying to get my daughter's shoes on, and I wave toward the several hundred open spaces in the practically deserted parking lot. The woman looks irate at this point, waving dramatically at the space near me. She honks several more times and finally swerves theatrically into the space beside my car, narrowly missing hitting the back door that is now shielding my child who still sits in her car seat. As she stomps out of her truck, I can hear her beginning to berate me for "being rude." When she gets around her vehicle, she notices that I have a child who is clearly the reason I'm standing randomly at my back door. All of a sudden, her tune changes slightly. Oh, she says, I didn't know you had a kid. Simply this, as she retreats quickly toward the Dillard's door. She is clearly an employee, as her uniform displays. But as I look at the nearly empty parking lot, I still cannot fathom why the woman is so upset. To park one more space over will add, what, two more steps to her walk? There are several hundred other spaces totally open, why it is so incredibly necessary that she park in that particular space will always be beyond me. I don't know why this woman is having that kind of morning. I have no idea why she cannot accept any other space, and I have no idea why the presence of my child alters her attitude after all the excessive drama that's just been displayed. But, I do pray for the woman when she's gone. I pray that her day gets better and that God will allow her a breath. Clearly, life is not good right now. I will never forget that lady. The behavior is crazy and uncalled for, but that just means there is something way deeper going on. I pray that I have the ability to show grace when I meet people in the future having those kinds of days, wherever that may be. I pray that if I am ever having that kind of day that I will be shown grace as well.

———-

We now call it the Pizza Hut Debacle of 2013. We're staying in Mississippi, starving after a long day in the car. We arrive at the church later than expected, get our overnight bags unloaded, and instantly plan on takeout pizza as a quick dinner option. After placing our order online, my husband leaves for the restaurant. It's already late, and we are already starving. An hour later, I am sitting on the couch about to eat my own arm, and I get a text message: "I am STILL waiting and don't even know if they've started our pizza yet. There are a lot of people here in line as well. It looks like none of the employees really know what they are doing. Orders are getting messed up, and customers are getting really irate." My husband tells me that a guy who is given the incorrect pizza is offered $10 cash by another person in line for the unwanted pie. Apparently all the customers are getting equally frustrated with the inept management of the business. After nearly another hour goes by and the pizzas are still not forthcoming, I get back online find a nearby Papa John's restaurant and make an order. My husband leaves the Pizza Hut to the madness of a brewing riot and finds our new order ready when he arrives at the Papa John's a few miles away. When he arrives back at the church to his family, it is more than two hours since he left. Our child is now about to go to bed, and I am about to eat the cardboard pizza shell. It is not a calm, relaxing scene when dinner finally appears. Okay, so we practically inhale what should have been thoroughly tasty and delicious splurge food. Oh no, our pang racked stomachs have disintegrated into barren wastelands of dry, cracked earth barely registering the cleansing, cheesy goodness that seeks to heal its desolation. Um, thank you, Papa John's, for rescuing our evening and bringing us back from the brink of distended bellies. Alright, we may have survived one evening without food, but that isn't the point. The point is that sometimes an evening winds up far more dramatic (read frustrating) than one expects. But, this story has a happy ending. Yes, that day ended with full stomachs, full of scrumptious pizza from the Papa. But, it gets better. Because of the utter lack of professionalism and, you know, job skills displayed at the local Pizza Hut, we took the time the next morning to post a review to the company website. We really just wanted to let them know that things were not being taken care of at that particular location and that customers were leaving in droves because of poor service. This review/complaint results in multiple complimentary pizza coupons that prove to be great blessings while we are out of the road over the next six months.

Yes, the Pizza Hut Debacle was a long night, but God supplied many other free dinners because of that one experience. I think He knows how to take care of His own in some amazing ways, even if it requires that we occasionally feel a bit put out in the process.

———-

In the 21st century, there are some amazing technological tools at the traveler's disposal. Portable GPS (global positioning system) is a tremendous help on deputation. A driver simply inputs any physical address, and the GPS provides a real time, mobile map to direct every turn and highway exit. We have often been very thankful for this little machine, as it has literally orchestrated countless cross country treks accurately and successfully. However, technology can be a blessing and a curse. All computers have their limitations. Throughout our years on the road, we have been directed to more than one empty field, dirt road, dead end, and closed business. When traveling, we learn quickly that a GPS isn't always accurate. It isn't always up to date. It isn't always trustworthy. The maps are only as good as the city's street and numbering system. One Sunday morning, the GPS led us to a TJ Maxx store, rather than the church for which we were searching (we found it about ten minutes later about 3 miles farther down the road after checking the church's website and the directions posted there). One day, we mapped to a Target store and, after a 40 minute drive, found a Wal-Mart in its place. That was crazy because even the yellow pages phonebook said it was a Target, but it was in fact a Wal-Mart. We've still never figured that one out. Once we were headed to a hotel up in Ohio. Its sign was clearly visible from the highway. But, the GPS told us to turn left after exiting rather than right in the direction of the sign. We thought it odd, but maybe it was a different hotel we were actually supposed to be in. We follow the GPS directive only to learn within the next two minutes that it is taking us in a giant loop right back to the highway and the hotel that we spotted before. Really? Oh yes. We have no idea what caused it to do that, but it did. And, that isn't the only time it has directed in a random, pointless loop. One time it instructed us to drive into a residential area, just to take us in a circle through the subdivision and back out onto the main road. I guess the GPS also stands for "going places screwily". Well, that's not exactly a word, but it fits at times. Yes, there have been moments where our GPS has simply been wrong. But overall, it truly is one of the best inventions for those of us living on the road traveling every day to new places.

———-

Meeting new people is literally an everyday occurrence for the deputation missionary. So, we get comfortable really quickly with any new environment, any new set of people and personalities. One situation that could be awkward but turned out quite nicely happens one night in Tennessee. We are driving through the state on our way to Florida. We need a place to stay for the evening, and one church that my husband phones tells us that they don't have their own mission apartment. But, the church does have families that will open their homes to missionaries traveling through the area. That evening we stay with one of those families. It seems a little odd at first, going to a perfect stranger's private home and staying in their basement guest room. But, the couple with two younger children is more than welcoming. We eat a nice dinner and sit around the living room talking, sharing, and watching the kids play together most of the evening. When we stay with strangers, the last thing we want to be is a burden of any kind. So we attempt to be as quiet and easy as possible. We always hope to leave a good impression and show our appreciation. Throughout deputation, we stay with several different people, and it has, thankfully, been mainly wonderful experiences. We have heard many horror stories about awkward or strange things encountered when staying in people's homes. But, God has been gracious to us. Each person who opens his or her home to a traveling missionary is a tremendous blessing, and we pray that each one is blessed greatly because of the hospitality shown.

———-

We are from the south, from Texas, where it is extra HOT most of the year. So, what do you do for free entertainment when it's too hot outside for a local playground or if you are in an area without a kids' park? Um, a local mall of course. What, you didn't know? Oh yes, shopping malls have begun to feature some pretty large and elaborate children's play areas. Climate controlled. Padded benches for the parents. Usually differing levels of climbing equipment and padded floors. We visit many of these free and open play areas throughout the country, most being quite pleasant experiences for both our daughter and us. One interesting aspect to visiting these malls though is the study in sociology that each affords. If any person wants to study a microcosm of parenting styles, personality traits, or societal expectations, he or she need only visit a children's play land that is open to the public and free for all. We get to observe many aspects to American culture, good and bad, in those locations. We have met many friendly people and adorable, smiling children. Our daughter has interacted with all kinds of children of both genders and played perfectly well alongside them. But, we have also observed many disturbing parenting trends and been on the receiving end of more than one toddler bully whose parents neither care nor pay enough attention to prevent their child from being rude to others.

One afternoon, my daughter (who isn't the most adventurous climber around) finds herself "stuck" in a play airplane. She'd climbed in just fine but couldn't determine how to get out. So rather than cry for help, she simply stands inside it and watches the other kids, enjoying the view. Cut to a few minutes later when two girls a couple years older than my toddler are racing around the area. Mini twisters causing chaos and leaving things demolished in their wake. Now, we've already seen these girls push other children and run into others, basically domineering everything and everyone in their path. So, our eyes are trained in their direction anyway. What happens next becomes an epic memory retold many times. The girls decide that THEY want to play in the plane and how dare this little imp toddler think she can stand within it. So initially they jump into the plane and begin ordering my daughter out, pushing on her shoulders in the process. This of course is highly disturbing to my child who is terrified of falling out of the plane, and her face begins to mirror her panic. Then, presumably because my daughter is not moving out of their way fast enough, the larger of the two girls physically picks up my child and tosses her over the edge, effectively ousting her from the plane. Now, as my daughter begins to sob, I step instantly over to them, picking my daughter off the ground and wondering why no parent is monitoring or correcting this girl's behavior. While trying to calm a little girl's torrent of tears, I tell the two bullies that they need to get out of the plane. No. No, I say. Get out. You are not going to play in here. The look they give me is disbelief. They have seemingly never heard the word no, which judging by their actions is probably true. They begrudgingly exit the plane and move to other areas of the play land. A cute baby boy (no more than a year old) toddles up to the plane and starts to climb on it. His mother quickly appears telling him no. I assure her that he is fine. After all, he is simply playing and has no intention of bullying anyone. Still no parent shows up. As things become calm and children go back to playing, I do spy three adults who apparently belong to these girls. They stand off to one side, talking to each other, texting on cell phones, and basically ignoring their children's behavior all together. That day is also supposed to be extra fun because we have friends meeting us with their son whose is one of our child's best friends. When our friends arrive, I let my friend know about the goings on and the resident spitfires. As I'm explaining what went down, we see the two bullies shove yet another child off a large plastic boulder in order to ascend the rock themselves. Wow! You see what I mean? But, that's not the end! Oh, there's more. So my friend's been warned, and our kids are having a fabulous time laughing and playing together. All is well...we think. The tornadoes are continuously swirling around the play area, having the affect you'd assume...momentary chaos wherever they touch. Our kids are standing in a corner, talking to each other, when all of a sudden the blonde and brunette storms barrel between them, the blonde literally knocking my friend's son to the ground and trampling over the top of him in her reckless, mindless pursuit of speed. In the course of this one play area visit, my child's been thrown to the ground, her best buddy's been stamped over, and nothing...I find myself staring at the blonde girl's mother, wondering if she's going to acknowledge this newest offence. Finally, after what seems an inordinate amount of time, I see the realization hit this woman that her child has somehow crossed a line. Yes, apparently NOW, the girl has crossed a line. Okay, NOW is the only time the woman is paying enough attention to what the child is doing in the first place. After much struggle, the woman pulls her daughter over and tells her to apologize to my friend and her son; the child utterly refuses, stomping her feet and yelling no and ultimately jerking out of her mother's grasp and running in the other direction. Goodness, it's difficult to know even how to respond. Shortly thereafter, the tiny tornadoes and accompanying adults leave, and peace resumes for everyone else. Shocking is the change in the atmosphere once these two little girls are gone. It often amazes me when I see parents use play areas or park playgrounds as babysitters, ignoring their kids for the duration of their visit. Our job is to guide our children in the right way, directing and correcting where needed. Children are natural sinners and know instinctively how to be selfish and rude and mean to others. Without parental guidance teaching children self-control and God's laws and expectations for their behavior, they will always become the worst versions of themselves. We have certainly had front row seats to parenting strategies that clearly don't incorporate God's standards and instructions. We've also been blessed to witness parenting stemming directly from God's principles and the blessings that ensue from them. Know that our children require our guidance. They require that we teach them the right way, God's way. This idea that kids left to themselves with no discipline will somehow become super wonderful, responsible, caring people is a fallacy of the devil, and anyone who takes even a few minutes to observe the world will find that obvious. Fight the good fight. Raise your children to honor the Lord in all that they do. We pray every day that God gives us the strength and wisdom to be the godly parents that our daughter deserves and needs us to be for her.

————-

Truckers spend hours, days, and weeks in their vehicles, driving day in and day out. But at the end of their run, they still go home. They still have somewhere to keep most of their "stuff." They still can travel pretty light. Most of us full-time deputation missionaries, however, have no home base. We literally live out of our cars 100% of the time. Our "stuff" is continuously surrounding us: Falling over the backseat, stuffed down into corners, hiding beneath the front seats, lining the edge of the baby's car seat, occasionally rolling underfoot. Sometimes it overtakes all available leg room and arm room. Sometimes we cannot get to items that we may need because they are buried underneath other things. Sometimes it just feels like a mess, a mess that we cannot get rid of no matter how many times it's organized and repacked and reorganized. Living in close quarters with all ones possessions can make tensions high on long days and can also make some things simpler. When our child's potty training isn't foolproof, we have all her changes of clothes right on hand; that's a plus. When we have no way to clean said accident laundry but must hold it within a few square feet of our persons for the remainder of an eight hour car ride, that's a minus. When the trashcan keeps tipping over requiring retrieval of used wet wipes, candy wrappers, and not quite empty soda cans, it does not exactly spell moment for a prayer meeting. Wait, maybe it does. Okay, yes, we have more reasons for impromptu prayer meetings than many, but maybe it's just because we are constantly being reminded of the weaknesses of human nature when we are in this constant state of movement. Thank God, this is a temporary aspect to being a missionary. After nearly three years on the road, we are ready for a home. We are ready to be out of the car. We are ready for a regular size trash can that sits neatly in the kitchen. We are ready for a different set of things that try our patience and test our faith's mettle. There will always be struggles. There will always be frustrations, but thank goodness, the U.S.S. Sorrento is about to retire. We are excited to embark on the starship home base, wherever God determines that should be. We're ready for new adventures that have nothing to do with leaving and everything to do with being where God has called us.

Chapter Five- Lessons Learned

I have only just finished this adventure known as full-time deputation. We have not yet landed on our field, on the soil that will become our new home. I am not the mother of a passel of children nor has our ministry yet opened the doors of a new church. I neither offer advice to those who have tread this road long before me nor feel as though my experience is indicative of every missionary's journey. I do, however, wish to be an encouragement to those seeking God's will in their lives, to those who know full-time ministry is their path, to those who just want to know more about what it's like to get started in this vocation, to those who are just curious, and to those who read and remember (whether fondly or not) their own deputation experiences. This awesome and amazing Sovereign God who created us teaches me new, inspiring, challenging, humbling things each and every day. I know that there is much to learn once we reach our field. I know that, regardless of "success" or "difficulty" on that field, I still have far more to learn about my Savior. God's Holy Word is full of God's attributes and His goodness! Verse after verse displays His majesty and veracity continuously.

One particular chapter, however, seems to encapsulate the main lessons that God taught me during deputation: Proverbs 3. You may remember those posters that used to be everywhere: "All that I learned about life, I learned from..." All that I learned about deputation, I learned from Proverbs 3.

Verse 3: "Let not mercy and truth forsake thee: bind them about thy neck; write them upon the table of thine heart." Because of God's mercy, He purposed to save us from our sins. Because of that truth, it is our honor to serve Him anywhere in any way, no matter what that service requires of us. Deputation does require constant faith in your call. Bind the truth of your call about your neck. Without utter faith in that, deputation is nearly impossible to complete.

Verse 5-6: "Trust in the Lord with all thine heart; and lean not unto thine own understanding. In all thy ways acknowledge Him, and He shall direct thy paths." Our human, finite minds cannot understand all the workings of an infinite God's will, but we DO know God. We know that He is trustworthy and constant, never failing, never wavering. He knows where He's going, and His GPS is always leading us in the right way. Following Him is the only way to know what the end result will actually be. Deputation is a quick way to discover the best and the worst from people who call themselves Christians. People may disappoint. People may steer you wrong. People may be the greatest blessing or the biggest disappointment. If your trust is in Him, the strength or frailty of human nature will not derail your direction.

Verse 7: "Be not wise in thine own eyes: fear the Lord, and depart from evil." This is the conclusion of the previous thought and the simplicity (though never easy) of our jobs as Christians. I learned that I have to realize that I am not wise and never will be compared to an omniscient God. I must put my reverence for Him above my own thinking. Being a true child of God is never easy, but real Christianity is simply this verse in a nutshell. Deputation comes with a lot of expectations. Many churches and pastors have many different standards and expectations, some good, some unique, some not even Biblical. Trying to meet all these expectations can drive the deputation missionary crazy. You may agree with these "rules;" you may not. This is the standard: It's not our wisdom but God's that matters. Does God give that standard? Yes, then great. That's a no-brainer. You should do it, no question. If not, do not let it cause anxiety. Let Him direct. Fear Him and eschew evil. These are the standards that are irrefutable. We certainly need to be appropriate and as non-offensive as possible. But, I have learned that one pastor's opinion does not a God's mandate make. We should never seek to justify our own thoughts for their own merit (we are not wise); we should, though, let God alone be true and every man a liar as Paul mentions in Romans.

Verse 9 and 10: "Honor the Lord with thy substance...So shall thy barns be filled with plenty..." Few people are as intimately acquainted with God's creative and abundant provision than those in full-time ministry. Deputation is no exception. Tithes and offerings are still our reasonable service to our home church, regardless of how much or little we are receiving while on deputation. Giving to our own church's mission program is also something God still expects from us. We have been faithful to this command, often marveling at how completely God has supplied all our needs (and many wants) no matter how little came in above what we were giving. Whether a random gift card, a generous love offering, a discount coupon, or a birthday present, ways to save money and extra income seemed to abound constantly. You truly cannot out give God, and He will not allow His children to be in want when we are following His directives for our finances. Period. Living love offering to love offering can be really tough; it can cause worry. There's horrid gas prices, hotel expenses, take out, and many other daily supplies needed. But, God! That's all we need to know.

Verse 13: "Happy is the man that findeth wisdom, and the man that getteth understanding." God is the author of all wisdom and understanding. Therefore, the closer we get to God, the happier we will inevitably be. It's really that simple, and that difficult. Happiness is a daily desire, so our pursuit of Him must likewise be a daily pursuit. We only find what we actually search for. In order to find wisdom, we have to look for it. God reveals His wisdom in His Word. We must start there every day, or we will always be lacking in happiness. Deputation can be a roller coaster of emotion, one day of total elation, one day in the depths of despair. One day you're on track with everything; the next, you're barely getting by. One day you've seen the hand of God; the next, you're trying to make sure you can even still hear His voice. On those days when we are frustrated, annoyed, grieving, angry, depressed, or simply unhappy, we MUST seek out His wisdom in order to understand our circumstance. When we allow God to reveal His ways, His goals, His agenda, we will always find the happiness that exists only in His wisdom, in His perfect and strong embrace.

Verse 19: "The Lord by wisdom hath founded the earth; by understanding hath He established the heavens." Everything rests on Him, on His wisdom. Deputation can be a waiting game. It can be a game of unwritten rules and unwritten expectations as far as churches and pastors are concerned. Missionaries meet many people throughout deputation that have far different "understandings" about things than what God lays out anywhere in Scripture. Sometimes on deputation, it can feel as though you are the only person trying to put into practice what God actually commands from His people. Though you may feel "in it alone," God knows what He's doing. He founded the earth and established the heavens by the power of His wisdom. He knows what each of us needs to learn and be prepared to handle. Deputation is a bit like a Litmus test. Those who understand that God knows what He's doing ALL the time, in EVERYTHING, will survive. Those who don't, may not.

Verse 23 and 24: "Then shalt thou walk in thy way safely, and thy foot shall not stumble. When thou liest down, thou shalt not be afraid: yea, thou shalt lie down, and thy sleep shall be sweet." These verses result from "keeping sound wisdom and discretion." During deputation, you stay in many different places, with many different people, in areas that are unknown and sometimes unsure. Some places feel safe; others really don't. But we learned that God truly does take care of us no matter where we may have to sleep, no matter what is going on around us. We need not ever worry because our safety is assured in Him.

Verse 27: "Withhold not good to them to whom it is due, when it is in the power of thine hand to do it." Deputation enables a missionary to be on the receiving end of this verse in some pretty amazing ways. I have myself been awed and blessed beyond imagination by the generosity and hospitality and love of God's people. We have been showered with gifts, had tanks of gas purchased, been provided with countless meals, been offered babysitting and laundry services, been invited to parties, and found ourselves lifted up by some pretty powerful prayer warriors. We try to take every opportunity that we have to do good to those around us, but deputation can feel often solitary. It's important to take those opportunities to be a blessing, and you will feel that verse lived out more so during deputation than just about any other time.

Verse 31: "Envy not the oppressor, and choose none of his ways." It isn't the easiest thing to admit, but deputation (like all full-time ministry jobs) can often feel like a treadmill, really difficult and ultimately going nowhere. Those times are especially used by the devil to put in your mind people who "seem" successful in their pursuits with none of your perceived difficulty yet do not seem to be upholding God's standards. Think of some famous "preachers" who make millions of dollars by NOT teaching the whole Word of God. Many times the devil will put in our minds that it's impossible to succeed without compromise. I know that this thought comes from the devil because it's an unequivocal lie from the pit of hell. God does not change; His Word does not change. His standards do not change. Therefore, following Him can never include compromise on His message or His Truth. God would not have warned us against envy if He wasn't aware of a plausible temptation. Yes, this world makes it difficult to "do it God's way" sometimes. Yes, some claiming Christianity make it difficult at times. In weak moments, we may wish that ministry wasn't fraught with challenges and find ourselves wishing that our ministry could mimic what we think we see in another's. But oftentimes, worldly success comes at the expense of our heavenly God. This is never an option. We must be very careful to take those thoughts captive and not allow them to take root in our hearts. God is very clear on the methodology for pleasing Him (think Cain and Abel's example). Unless we do it God's way, we cannot be blessed, even if the devil wants us convinced otherwise. It's easy to want to begin making comparisons when on deputation, comparisons with other missionaries about support level and duration of travel and miles crossed or states visited. It's easy to feel less than when you hear of another who seems to have an easier time getting bookings or easy to feel puffed up if God clears a path for you that isn't open to another. These comparisons are often compounded by the fact that many churches and pastors also flaunt these comparisons. We've had those who've said that there isn't a reason why our deputation should take longer than one year when another missionary could raise his support within one year. Often these comparisons are clearly apples and oranges. Only you know if you are doing things God's way. If you are, please don't be discouraged. Fast or slow, God's ways are not ours, but they are best. He's proven that over and over again throughout every moment of history. The devil would have us believe that doing things like the ungodly will somehow produce success that following God will not. God's warnings are always needful, and deputation can certainly weary the soul. This is why we must be aware of the devil's lies and choose not to take his messages seriously.

Verse 34: "Surely He scorneth scorners: but He giveth grace unto the lowly." Sadly, deputation also provides ample opportunity for people to question God's call on the missionary's life. What is truly from God will be evident to any and all people who seek Him. I mean, by that, that people who question a call solely for the sake of dismissing a missionary will be responded to by God in kind. Likewise, those who wish to know God's will are made privy to it. What happens to those who are not interested in God's call or His plan for saving this world is not our concern. He will take care of those people. We need not scorn the scorners, for He will do that Himself. On deputation, we meet countless people who can tell instantly that we are real and genuine, truly seeking to serve God on the mission field. God promises grace to those who submit themselves to Him, grace to the missionary who is submitted and grace to the local church member who is submitted equally to His plan.

Basically, deputation (whether long or short) is a time for testing and teaching, adapting and surviving, blessing and being blessed. It is a wonderful journey of exploration and submission. It begins by being submitted to our immutable, almighty God; it ends with continued submission to the One who saved us, redeemed us, called us, and cares for us with every breath we take. We are so thankful that deputation is temporary, but we must be careful to apply the lessons learned for the rest of our lives!

###

A Note from the Author:

Thank you so much for reading my little memoir! As a mother of a toddler and heading to the foreign field as a church planting missionary, I know that my little girl won't remember the people or places that we have visited during these travels, but I wanted to record the incredible journey that God took us on for her to learn about when she gets older as well as for our own reminiscence. But I pray that these little tales will make you laugh and make you think and also help you to know even more the incredible power of the God we serve. I pray it was a blessing to you! Everything we encounter in life is meant to make us better equipped for His service. Live each day with that in mind, and you will know blessing around each bend (even if the bed is really uncomfortable and the train whistle is piercing your ears). God Bless!

Also check out my series of children's stories: **The Littlest Missionary Series**, also available free from Smashwords[1] and other ebook retailers.

I would love to hear your feedback on this or other stories in my collection! Please send any comments or questions to **browns2australia@yahoo.com**. Thank you so much!

---

1.   https://www.smashwords.com/profile/view/MABrown77974

Did you love *Confessions of a Deputation Missionary*? Then you should read *Hope I See...*[2] by Melissa Brown!

Can Hope be seen in this world?

Can poetry unveil Hope to the human heart, making the invisible visible?

...words like watercolors
cascading across the page,
shaded tones of nuance
and perspective crafted
by imagery hawking its wares,
spirit and life expressed
with no less grace than
a prima ballerina on stage,

---

2. https://books2read.com/u/mZg5pD

3. https://books2read.com/u/mZg5pD

perfect poems paint portraits
but in terms and tears
soaking the page,
in rage, in love, in passion, in power,
in poetry!
Come take a look inside and see the wonders of Hope...
(approx. 125 pages)

Also by Melissa Brown

Sensing a Saviour
Hope I See...

Standalone
The Littlest Missionary
Jael Learns the "Bee" Attitudes
Jael Learns the Ten Commandments
Jael Learns to Listen
Jael's Christmas Spirit
Confessions of a Deputation Missionary
Jael Travels the Romans Road
Jael Learns the Power of 'No'

About the Author

Melissa Brown is a native Texan, wife, mother, English teacher, ministry leader, and pastor's kid who has always loved the beauty of words, a good story, and the art of the "telling." Having been in all different ministries most of her life around the USA and Australia, she finds purpose in all of life's sun and shadows and longs to share God's grace and Truth through the art He inspires.